Oldest Mom
ON THE
PLAYGROUND

JUDY HAVESON

Also written by Judy Haveson
Laugh Cry Rewind – A Memoir

J Press Books

First Edition September 24, 2024

Cover Design by Laura Kicinski & Lucy Lewis

Author Photo by Adam Cohen

ISBN: 979-8-9866249-5-2 (print)

Printed in United States of America

To Adam and Jack
Thank you for allowing me to tell our stories.
I love you forever.

Author's Note

BECOMING A MOTHER OVER forty doesn't make me unique or special; it makes me a statistic. And tired. I decided to share my forty-something journey to motherhood and beyond to show other women like me they're not alone on the ride and that age doesn't define the love and laughter found in parenthood. I'm certainly not perfect, so I give no advice, and I've made many mistakes through the years. I challenge you to show me a mother who always gets it right.

I wrote this book as a series of stand-alone essays, so you don't have to read them in order. All the stories are based solely on my memory, and since I haven't slept a whole night's sleep since my son was born, I may have used some creative licensing. Some of the essays did not happen precisely as I wrote them, some dialogue has been recreated, and some names have been changed to protect the privacy of those involved.

Motherhood at any age is challenging. But as Erma Bombeck once said, "When the going gets tough, the tough make cookies." I'll add, just make sure you don't eat them in one sitting all alone.

Enjoy, and thank you for reading!

Contents

Introduction

I Want a Dog

WHEN I WAS IN MY late twenties, I wanted a dog. My then-boyfriend, whom I thought I'd marry, said, "You can barely take care of yourself; you're not ready to take care of a dog."

We broke up shortly after.

He was right, but how those words stung. Even over the next several years, as I learned to care for myself and built a successful communications and public relations career, his words echoed in my head. My clock ticked further and further away from my twenties. I felt as if I lived on The Game of Life board, driving around, collecting a paycheck, and choosing a career path over family. My little car sat empty with no husband and no blue or pink pegs. When I entered my thirties, I realized I wanted a family and a dog.

While in my late twenties / early thirties, my life was about having fun, listening to rock 'n roll, and building my career. I lived independently, worked, and paid bills; that's all I did for myself. I took my laundry to my parents' house every weekend for my mother to handle.

"Do you even know how to do laundry?" my father asked.

"Yes, I know how to do my laundry. But Mama does it so much better than me," I said.

And she did.

While my father teased me, I knew my mother loved caring for her little girl. Who was I to argue or stand in her way?

I also possessed limited cooking skills and the sparse kitchen setup to prove it.

Hannah, one of my closest friends, said, "Haveson, you have nothing in your refrigerator but water, batteries, and frozen chicken that looks like it's been there for months. How do you feed yourself?"

"Cooking has never been my thing. But I make great reservations," I joked.

While living my best life, my friends (including Hannah) were walking down the aisle, and I amassed a vast collection of colorful bridesmaid dresses and matching shoes. And then everyone started having babies. I'd be lying if I said I didn't suffer from FOMO. I feared I was missing out on marriage and children. I feared I was being left behind because I'd waited too long. Yet I continuously thought, *I'll have this one day too, right?*

I always fashioned myself a late bloomer, and not solely based on my timeline for marriage and having a family. Yes, I wanted marriage, a family, a career—and a dog. But I never felt ready. I was focused on finding myself and my purpose.

It would have been easy to blame everything on the tragedies and losses in my life: experiencing sexual assault at age twelve, living through multiple health issues with my parents, and losing my sister, Celia, to cancer. Any of my life experiences could have left me in the fetal position, never wanting to get out there and make something of myself. I could have gotten angry at the world for ruining what I believed to be an everyday existence. But that would be playing the victim card, something I vowed never to do.

The real reason for my hesitancy is this: I was scared. I was frightened to live my life, fearful that something terrible would happen if I let my guard down. This theory, unfortunately, is how life conditioned me. The most significant example of this thinking is when I lost Celia. She was twenty-six when she died; I was nineteen. Her death left me paralyzed, and I often wondered how I could move forward with my life, much less find purpose or happiness without her.

Before Celia died, she wrote me a letter encouraging me to keep going, even after she was gone.

"Judy, promise me when the time comes, I don't want you to change, and I want you to continue being your smart and funny self," she wrote.

She made me promise that her death wouldn't mean I'd stop living and following my dreams. But that's the thing; I didn't know what my dreams were in my twenties and thirties. I moved from Texas to California, back to Texas, and eventually to New York, trying to find myself. I built a successful career in radio broadcasting, music promotions, and public relations. I lived my life one day at a time. Then I hit my late thirties and realized I wanted to stop moving. I wanted to settle down and build something more than a career. I wanted a husband, children, and a dog.

Unfortunately, I didn't have an excellent dating track record. Never one to pass on a free meal, I went on many first dates but few second ones. One such first/last date example was with a guy named Matthew. While living in Austin, Texas, I entered the cyber-dating world. Matthew became my first online date. We met at Trudy's, a trendy Austin joint known for its margaritas.

Hey, I might as well feel no pain while going through what will probably be the most painful experience of my life.

They say every picture tells a story. According to the outdated photo posted on Matthew's dating profile, he had something in his story to hide. I have no problem with men who are hair challenged. Some bald men are very handsome. Including my dad. But what was he thinking by posting a picture from at least fifteen years prior? Did he think I wouldn't notice? Hell, he should have just posted his bar mitzvah picture. At least that would have been funny.

But Matthew's outdated photo is a close second to the best part of the meeting. As I walked toward him after arriving at the restaurant, I noticed a pin on the lapel of his ski jacket. Upon further inspection I figured out it was Eeyore, the donkey from *Winnie the Pooh*. While I fondly like Mickey Mouse, I don't wear him on a first date. Thinking the date had nowhere to go but up, I approached the rest of the evening with the positive thought that I'd soon be chugging down the fabulous margarita I'd been dreaming about all day.

I'm not sure what happened next, but I remember the wait to be seated was too long, Matthew was hungry, and we left to walk down the street to eat at El Patio, a famous Tex-Mex dive in Austin. The good news was that it would be a very short evening since El Patio nuked all their meals.

Somewhere between the puffed chili con queso appetizer and the cheese enchiladas, I learned Matthew had recently stopped practicing law to return to school and get his master's in library administration.

"I think the legal profession is a joke," he said. "I can get more out of life by checking books out to law students and telling them to drop out of law school while they still have the chance."

What an uplifting and cheerful guy Eeyore turned out to be. While I could hardly wait to learn more, I decided to leave Eeyore, Piglet, and Christopher Robin at the House at Pooh Corner and never look back.

I continued my part-time dating job after I moved to New York City in 2001, with similar results. This job became more exhausting than my full-time career in public relations. After a wild plethora of dates, I decided to take a break. During my hiatus, a guy named Adam contacted me on Jdate, the online dating site for Jewish singles. A few months before I turned thirty-eight, and he turned forty, we met for a drink. Shortly after that first drink, we became inseparable.

I hadn't met anyone like Adam before. He gave me stability in a way I couldn't ever imagine, especially after suffering so much heartache and loss in my earlier years. While I'd met several men when I first moved to New York City (online and off-line), none felt like someone I wanted to spend the rest of my life with. Until Adam. And not only because he cooked. But that fact did help seal the deal. Also, my sarcastic humor seemed a great counterbalance to his serious nature.

We dated for a year before he asked me to marry him. While we dated, we'd often talk about our future, where we'd live, and whether kids were part of our plan. Adam and I married when I was forty, and he was forty-two. We never spoke out loud about "trying" to get pregnant or put a timeline in place for it to happen, but I secretly wondered if my body would cooperate and if I could even get pregnant in my forties.

According to babycenter.com, a forty-year-old woman has about a 40 to 50 percent chance of getting pregnant each year. Comparatively, a woman in her mid-thirties has about a 75 percent chance each month. But by age forty-three, a woman's chance of getting pregnant within a year drops significantly to 1 to 2 percent.

Motherhood finally happened to me at forty-three. Clearly, I defied the odds.

As older moms, we've lived a lifetime, and our experiences will only help guide us and build a stronger bond with our children. By association, having a child later in life can make you feel younger too. You'll still feel inadequate, guilty, and every bit of your advanced age daily. But as Erma Bombeck, one of my all-time favorite authors, said, "Children make your life important." She also said, "Insanity is hereditary. You can catch it from your kids." There's definitely a good argument for both thoughts.

The following collection of essays is my take on motherhood after forty. From suffering multiple pregnancy losses, to finally carrying to term, to leaving the career I'd spent years building to stay home and raise a child in New York City, to becoming a card-carrying member of the sandwich generation while navigating the loss of a parent, I chronicle my journey and showcase my realities, sadness, failures, insecurities, and triumphs as an "older" mom. I give no parenting advice, only personal reflection. And I take nothing in my life for granted.

My message to other women like me is to embrace the title of "oldest mom on the playground" and let go of the guilt and insecurities. And don't worry that your breasts aren't as perky as they used to be or that you have more wrinkles than the younger moms (that can be fixed). Wear it all like a badge of honor. Just pray that when you're surrounded by other moms at a class event or an eight-year-old's birthday party, no one mistakes you for the grandmother.

Midlife Mama

Pregnant at Forty, Forty-one, and Forty-two …

SIX WEEKS AFTER ADAM broke the ceremonial glass under the chuppah and we smashed our wedding cake in each other's faces, I peed on a stick and stared in disbelief when I saw the two pink lines. At the age of forty, I was pregnant.

How can I be pregnant so soon? We still need to order our wedding pictures.

At first, I misread the directions and thought the two lines meant I wasn't pregnant. This mistake made me realize that my forty-year-old eyes would require reading glasses to see the tiny print from then on.

"Adam, come here. I need to show you something," I said, dragging him away from the kitchen where he was preparing a delicious meal for dinner.

"Okay, okay, I'm coming," he said. "Let me turn down the heat so I don't burn the fish."

As I pulled him toward the bathroom, he stopped me before we walked through the door.

"You're pregnant?" he guessed.

"Yes," I said with a big smile. "Are you shocked?"

"How, I mean, wow!" he said.

While we weren't seriously trying yet, we were newlyweds.

"Do you think we're ready for this?" I asked.

"I guess we'll find out soon," he said.

I'm confident those exact words are uttered by every soon-to-be-parent when they find out a baby is on the way. Truth: I was more than ready to become a mother. This had been a dream of mine ever since my parents bought me the Sunshine Family Treehouse playset for Hanukkah in 1974. These anti-Barbie dolls included Steve, Stephie, and their baby, Sweets. They lived in a foldable treehouse. I wished I lived in it too.

But Steve and Stephie didn't wait until they turned forty to marry each other and start a family. By the time they reached my age, they were probably grandparents and had downsized and retired to a smaller treehouse in Florida, on a golf course. The same can be said for some of my girlfriends. While they didn't live in treehouses, or on a golf course in Florida, they did get married and have children before I did. And while Adam and I were about to welcome a new baby into our family, many of our friends would soon be grandparents. I certainly didn't live my life being jealous of what others had, but I did long to get married and create a family.

I couldn't wait to have this baby. I thought about all the fun things we'd do, like exploring New York City, playing in Central Park, going to the beach, visiting family and friends, and traveling the world together. This baby would know nothing but love and adventure.

That night I took six pregnancy tests, all of which confirmed I was indeed pregnant. Then I decided we should stock up on parenting reading material.

"I need to buy a copy of *What to Expect When You're Expecting* tonight so I learn everything I can before the baby is born," I said.

After dinner that evening, we went to our neighborhood Barnes & Noble to get the book. Long before the invention of the Kindle or Apple Books, one of our favorite activities included going to the bookstore and buying new books to read over the weekend. While

Adam preferred nonfiction political and business books, I gravitated to chic lit and mysteries. I didn't know what floor housed the parenting section.

"It's not that I didn't think we'd eventually buy parenting books, but did you ever think we'd come here to browse the parenting section so quickly after we got married?" I asked.

"No, I didn't," Adam said, as we rode up the escalator to the third floor.

After I found the pregnant woman's bible, I perused the shelves of other books on everything from what to name your baby to how to get them to sleep. But I noticed one missing topic.

"Excuse me," I said to the salesperson. "Where's the book that tells you how to be a parent?"

She laughed. I didn't.

. . .

Over the next several weeks, I read everything I could about the early stages of pregnancy. I learned why I felt like crap, what to expect each week, and that the baby was no larger than an acorn. Then, the time came for the first sonogram. Adam and I would finally see a picture of our baby. I couldn't wait to meet my little acorn.

The technician led Adam and me to the examination room, where the sonogram would be taken.

"Change into this gown, and I'll return in a few minutes. Soon, you'll see the first pictures of your baby," she said.

I turned to Adam and gave him a big smile. I was nervous and excited at the same time, and so was he.

"Are you ready for this?" I asked him.

"As ready as I'll ever be," he said.

The technician re-entered the room. She squirted gooey, warm gel on my stomach and spent several minutes moving the wand over my belly. After squinting at the screen, she called for the doctor. The doctor came into the room and stared intently at the monitor.

"It appears there may be an issue, and we'd like you to come back next week so we can do another ultrasound to give us a baseline. The baby might have a chromosomal issue such as Down syndrome. You'll have to consider if this is something you can handle, but we'll know more next week," the doctor said.

I was speechless. Out of all the pregnancy books and magazine articles and internet searches, nothing had prepared me for the doctor telling us there might be a chromosomal issue. Or maybe I had decided not to read the countless articles discussing this possibility in older women.

With tears in my eyes, I turned to Adam and grabbed his hand.

"I'm scared. What if we lose the baby?" I asked.

"Let's not worry until we know everything. I'm scared too, but it will be okay," he said, squeezing my hand.

Sadly, before we got to the following week's ultrasound, the baby died. A piece of me died too. When you wait almost half your lifetime to have a family and then something goes wrong, it's hard to imagine it's not your fault. Of course, this is illogical thinking, but it's difficult to think straight when you have a miscarriage.

A few days later, I had a D&C. The test confirmed the baby had Down syndrome, but I blamed myself.

I cried for a week.

The doctor told us we could try again once I healed.

"Should we try again?" I asked Adam. "I don't know if I can handle it if we lose another baby."

"Let's talk about it once you're feeling better," he said.

That's the thing; would I ever feel better after this loss? Even though I was no stranger to loss, losing a baby—my baby—felt different.

But we kept trying. I became pregnant again at age forty-one. That pregnancy also resulted in miscarriage. This time in my bathroom.

"I'm so sorry. I don't know why this happened again," I cried to Adam.

"It's not your fault. Everything is going to be okay," he said, assuring me.

Just like the previous pregnancy loss, I felt defeated. But I knew life would go on. And it did.

A few months later, I became pregnant again. I didn't miscarry, but there was no baby. I had a condition known as a blighted ovum, where your body produces the pregnancy hormone and creates a sac, but the baby never develops. The third pregnancy happened exactly one year after the first one. I found myself in the same hospital getting another D&C.

This can't be happening, and it's not my fault.

Suffering three consecutive pregnancy losses took a massive toll on my body and mind. And while I hurt, Adam hurt too. Pregnancy loss can be more difficult for the husband to process since they don't have to endure the physical pain. Adam may have felt helpless in my misery and sorrow, but he was anything but. He was my rock and kept me grounded.

Getting pregnant at age forty overwhelmed me. Suffering multiple pregnancy losses in one year gutted me. I couldn't help but think this was God's way of telling me I waited too long and wasn't ready for a dog.

. . .

A few weeks after the third pregnancy loss, I made an appointment with my doctor to discuss my options.

"What else should I do?" I asked Dr. Levine, my OB-GYN. "I feel like my old body has failed me."

"Judy, these things happen to women of all ages. You may need to give your body a rest," he assured me.

When I returned to my office, I called Adam to tell him about my conversation with Dr. Levine.

"I spoke to Dr. Levine today about all the pregnancy losses. He told me to stop putting pressure on myself about getting pregnant and relax."

"He's not wrong," Adam said.

While I desperately wanted a child, I wasn't fond of the process consuming my every thought. I wanted to enjoy my life with Adam, whether that included a baby or not. No matter how old you are when trying to have a child, getting pregnant becomes your sole focus. But being in my forties, I had the added pleasure of work obligations, marriage responsibilities, aging parents with health issues, and a fast-ticking hormonal clock running out of time. My plate was full.

"I need a 'me' plan," I told Adam. "And I need to take my mind off getting pregnant."

That was when I met Jenny, a personal trainer, who forever changed my life. While Adam and I belonged to a gym and regularly exercised, I'd never worked with a professional trainer. Jenny is a force of nature. Her small five-foot-three frame packs a mean punch and she takes no prisoners when it comes to personal fitness.

At each week's training session, Jenny incorporated a variety of exercises, including squats, burpees, lunges, deadlifts, and other pain-inducing routines that made me feel like vomiting. But these sessions shaped my body and mind and helped me realize my potential.

"You want me to do what? I can't do that!" I found myself saying each week, after she introduced a new exercise.

"You can and you will. It's mind over matter," Jenny said.

After several months, my mind started playing tricks on me because I began enjoying the torture. I was stronger, physically and mentally. Miraculously, I became pregnant for the fourth time at age forty-two, less than a year after I began my "me" journey. I felt excited, anxious, and overwhelmed. I'd seen this movie three different times, and I hoped this time would have a better ending. I prayed that the pregnancy gods would be with me. If they were, I'd be a forty-three-year-old first-time mother.

The night I broke the happy news to Adam, we went out to dinner. Not to celebrate, since that never seemed to work for us. Instead, we cautiously talked about our excitement for this pregnancy going to full-term.

"This time, it's going to work. I feel it in my bones," I told Adam.

"Me too," he said.

"My body is more prepared now. I've never been this strong or healthy."

"And you've never looked better," he said with a smile.

I kept hearing Jenny's words in my head: mind over matter. My mind got my body through the intense exercise routines I thought would break me. And I knew my mind could move my body to get through this new pregnancy with no issues.

After spending a year with Jenny, I'd never felt better about my body and myself. I would stand in front of my floor-length mirror and say, "I don't look bad for a forty-two-year-old!" I was proud of myself. But now that I was pregnant, I worried if I could keep it up and keep up with Jenny. Would I hurt my baby by pounding it out at the gym? Would Jenny go easier on me now that I was pregnant?

The answer to all my questions was a resounding no. My doctor said continuing my intense workout routine wouldn't hurt the baby. And Jenny definitely didn't go easier on me. In some ways, she was harder on me. And I'll forever be grateful for that.

I was still scared of suffering another loss. How couldn't I be? Adam was worried as well. How couldn't he be? But no matter the outcome, we had each other. And that's all that mattered.

You're Not Fat, You're Pregnant

THE EUPHORIC FEELING OF being pregnant came to a screeching halt the first time I strapped on a fake baby bump to try on maternity clothes. While I've never been a slave to fashion trends, I do like to look nice. But being five foot three, average weight for my height, endowed in the chest area, and cursed with the family trait of wide hips, buying clothes is always hit or miss. I'm consistently between sizes in most pants, dresses, and shirts. In other words, buying clothes is frustrating.

The anticipation of buying maternity clothes overwhelmed me. I didn't know how much weight I'd gain, or how much my boobs, ass, and hips would expand. While I wanted to buy age-appropriate clothes, I didn't want to look matronly. Nor did I want my big belly and wide ass on full display. My goal was to camouflage my baby bump, not accentuate it.

I couldn't ask my girlfriends for hand-me-downs since they'd either given their maternity relics away or burned them years before. I remembered most of their maternity clothes as unfashionable: high collars, solid colors, lots of big bows. Maternity fashion trends from the '90s were different from the '00s. Secretly, I was never jealous of their maternity clothes, so I didn't mind they couldn't give them to me.

. . .

One evening after work, I dropped into Destination Maternity at the corner of Madison Avenue and East 57th Street in Midtown Manhattan. After speaking to many of my mom friends, I learned that this one-stop shopping maternity mega store carried clothing for all occasions and in various price points. When I walked inside, I noticed many beautiful and stylish selections displayed at the front.

"How can I help you?" the lovely saleswoman asked me. "Are you looking for anything particular?"

"I'm looking for something to wear to work. My normal pants are super tight now," I replied.

"How far along are you?" she asked, sizing me up. "And what is your budget?"

"I'm about five months along now. And I hadn't thought about a budget."

The "no budget" response perked her up.

"Follow me. Let me show you some beautiful collections perfect for a work wardrobe."

I perused the clothing racks and found the clothes weren't as hideous as I expected. Since we were nearing summer, I noticed soft jersey knit tops, colorful sundresses, stylish business suits, and silk blouses. And then I saw the price tags.

"Oh my goodness," I exclaimed. "I had no idea how expensive maternity clothes were." Every outfit I saw cost more than anything hanging in my closet.

"Maternity clothes are fashionable today and rival styles you find in all the high-end department stores and boutiques," she explained.

"But where are the less expensive clothes I'll probably toss after the baby is born?" I asked.

She didn't like my question.

"We do have a section in the back of the store with racks of *those* items," she said with a snark.

After that response, she left me. The back section of the store looked like an island of mismatched maternity clothes. While the front of the store was beautifully curated, the back housed racks and racks of random pants, dresses, shirts, and loungewear. The clothes were smushed together so tightly I could barely pry them free. The pieces I managed to access and try on weren't flattering to my body and made me look like I was wearing a tent.

I stood before the floor-length mirror and held up a big polyester floral wrap dress. It reminded me of curtains. Next, I held up a pair of enormous stretchy pants. It looked as if I could fit my entire body in one leg. I had no idea what I needed or what size to try on, so I walked out of the store in tears.

. . .

I turned to Hannah and Carmen, two mom friends my age, to help me in my quest to find clothes. Hannah, a fashionista and mother to three daughters, is one of my closest friends. We met when I was nineteen and she was twenty-one. Through Hannah, I met Carmen, a former fashion retail executive, wardrobe stylist, and mother of three children. If there were people who could help me look stylish and cute as my body expanded, it was Hannah and Carmen.

While on the phone with Hannah one afternoon, I asked if she and Carmen would take me shopping for maternity clothes.

"I don't know what I'm doing," I whined. "I need help."

"We'll go to Target," she said.

"What? Target sells maternity clothes?"

"Yes, and the clothes are super cute, much better than when Carmen and I were pregnant," Hannah said. "And affordable."

Hannah and Carmen lived in Connecticut. One June after-noon, Adam and I drove to meet them at their swim club. Adam volunteered to stay with their kids while they took me to Target.

"You sure you've got this?" I asked Adam.

"Yes, it will be good practice," he said.

Fortunately, all the kids were excellent swimmers and needed little supervision.

At Target, we grabbed a shopping basket and Hannah and Carmen went to work. They grabbed soft T-shirts, lightweight sweaters, a variety of pants, including leggings and those with an adjustable waist, pj's made from knit jersey material, and cotton and knit dresses. They filled the cart with enough clothes for two pregnancies.

"I'm only going to be pregnant until November. Do I need all these clothes? And what size am I? What happens when I gain more weight? Will I have to buy more?" I asked, barely taking a breath.

I was so overwhelmed. Carmen entered the dressing room with me while Hannah filled my basket with more clothes.

"Put on this baby bump. It will help you know what size you'll be at different times during your pregnancy," Carmen said.

I looked in the mirror and screamed.

"I'm going to be this big?"

They both laughed at me.

"You have no idea," they said.

When I finished trying on everything they selected, I had enough clothes to last at least three or four months. The final price rivaled about two outfits from the store on Madison Avenue.

By my seventh month, I could barely look at the clothes I'd been wearing. You can only wear the same black tights and solid color tunics for so long. And everything was getting tight.

"I'm fat and need new clothes again," I told Adam.

"You're not fat. You're pregnant," he said.

Adam got me, and I loved him for it.

"We can go to Target and buy more clothes for you, but why don't we go back to Destination Maternity and you can pick out a few nice outfits to make yourself feel better about how you look," he said. "Even though you look beautiful to me, regardless of what you wear."

And so I returned to the overpriced maternity clothing store—this time with Adam. He encouraged me to select a few outfits.

"I hope we don't run into the same salesperson who helped me the last time I was here. But if we do, she'll probably be happy seeing you with me, guaranteeing her commission," I said.

It was fall, so I selected a few stretchy sweater dresses, black and brown wool pants, and long-sleeved blouses and T-shirts. Even though these items were technically maternity clothes, I could imagine incorporating them into my after-baby work wardrobe.

"Since it will probably take months to get my forty-something body back in shape, at least I'll have these beautiful clothes to keep wearing through the winter months. It's amazing how great you feel in stylish clothes that fit," I said.

"Happy wife, happy life," Adam said.

Nesting

I ALWAYS THOUGHT THE TERM "nesting" referred to birds. But I soon learned the word was synonymous with a mother-to-be preparing for the arrival of her baby. This meant getting all her affairs in order at the office and buying endless supplies, clothes, toys, and everything else needed for a newborn before the baby's arrival.

In October 2007, my friend Hannah hosted a baby shower at her home. Melinda, my best friend from childhood, and her husband, Steven, traveled to New York from Houston for the shower. Before the party, she took me shopping to begin my official nesting phase. What did I know about baby things? Melinda had birthed three children; as far as I was concerned, her expertise outshined mine by a mile. Like Hannah and Carmen outfitting me with stylish maternity clothes, I again benefited from a good friend's wisdom to guide me on my motherhood journey.

"I have several onesies and blankets," I proudly told Melinda. "I need to pick up a few other things to have ready for when the baby comes home, but I think I'm set."

She looked at me with the most mocking grin I'd ever seen and said, "A few things? You must be kidding?"

I wasn't. And apparently, neither was Melinda.

We went to Buy Buy Baby, the perfectly named store since every time someone walked through the sliding glass door entrance, they did nothing but buy, buy, and buy more than they probably needed. We each grabbed a shopping basket and walked up and down every aisle like contestants on Supermarket Sweep.

"Judy, you're going to need two to three of almost everything I show you," she told me.

"I don't understand the purpose of three sheet protectors, seeing as I'll only have one child," I said, questioning her.

"When you have to wake up in the middle of the night to change wet sheets, including this sheet protector, you'll thank me for having an extra. Trust me," she said.

And it didn't stop at sheet protectors. As I followed her with my cart, she kept throwing items into it: an ear thermometer, nasal aspirator, bottle warmer, multiple sleep sacks, syringes, nail clippers, five different salves, lotions, powders, rash creams, a vaporizer, a baby monitor, and more. When we reached the checkout counter, it looked like we had cleaned out the store.

"How many babies are you having?" the cashier asked me.

"I know, right?" I said, turning to Melinda with a cynical look on my face. "My friend swears I'll need all these items even though I'm birthing one baby."

"She doesn't realize it now, but she'll thank me later," Melinda told the cashier.

Adam and Steven eventually joined us as we were checking out of the store.

"Is there anything left on the shelves?" Adam asked me, looking at the twenty shopping bags sitting in our carts.

"Melinda swears we need it all," I said.

"Welcome to my world," Steven said with a laugh.

Because we lived in Manhattan, every store offered a delivery service—for an extra fee. And it's a good thing; otherwise, we would have needed a moving van to get everything home.

"Is our next stop the liquor store to stock up on must-need items for Adam and me?" I asked somewhat jokingly.

. . .

The following day, we gathered at Hannah's home for my baby shower. My friends and I were treated to champagne (I had one glass), and fantastic food and yummy desserts, including cookies Adam baked and decorated into the shape of baby bottles and carriages.

"Okay, let's gather around so Judy can open her gifts," Hannah said.

Everyone oohed and aahed as I opened gift after gift. I received blankets, onesies, stuffed animals, books, bath towels, a vibrating chair, an infant carrier, bottle warmers, musical mobiles, and more.

Oh great, more stuff for the baby.

I couldn't imagine where I'd find room for these baby items. Fortunately, we'd recently moved to a larger apartment with an extra bedroom and closet.

"It's a good thing we moved to a three-bedroom unit," I told Adam. "Otherwise, where would we put the kid?"

When we got home from the baby shower, I stood in the middle of the apartment and laughed hysterically as I surveyed all the gifts. I was the queen of moving and a regular at Bed Bath & Beyond, Target, and every other home goods store selling must-need items for a new home. But preparing for the arrival of a new baby took hoarding to a new level.

"We're going to need to rent another apartment for the baby's stuff. Or get a larger storage locker," I told Adam.

I didn't understand the purpose of multiple sheet protectors, dozens of onesies, and duplicates of almost every other baby supply that now sat in my closet. But a few weeks into the exhausting world of motherhood, I got it. One evening, I woke up at 2:00 a.m. to change Jack's sheets (and the sheet protector), just as Melinda had predicted. From that moment on, I never doubted Melinda's motherhood wisdom!

A Full Moon Labor

AS A CHILD OF the seventies, I learned a lot about pregnancy from watching reruns of *I Love Lucy*, *The Dick Van Dyke Show*, and *Bewitched*. Lucy Ricardo, Laura Petrie, and Samantha Stephens always craved pickles and ice cream, so naturally, I thought I'd have the same craving. But pickles and ice cream became the last things I could think of eating. Instead, I craved Jelly Belly jelly beans and candy corn.

October 2007 marked my eighth month of pregnancy. Halloween and all its decorations and candy dominated the stores. My access to candy corn was unlimited, but Jelly Belly candy proved more difficult to find.

"I don't want regular jelly beans. I'm craving Jelly Bellies," I told Adam when he handed me a package he bought at the drugstore.

While a jelly bean is a jelly bean, I yearned for the different flavors of Jelly Belly candies, such as Coca-Cola, Root Beer, Dr Pepper, piña colada, margarita, and bubble gum.

"The only place I can find Jelly Belly beans is Dylan's Candy Bar on Third Avenue and East Sixtieth Street," I told Adam when I called him at the office. "Will you please meet me after work, and then we can go to dinner?"

Call it a mission or obsession. Whatever you call it, I was desperate for Jelly Belly jelly beans.

Adam met me at Dylan's, and I became a kid in a candy store.

"Let's buy extra in case I run out," I said. (Unbeknownst to me, my best friend, Melinda, who lives in Houston, sent me a large box of Jelly Belly candy a few days later. I never ran out.)

That mid-October fall night Adam and I went to Dylan's was crisp and chilly, so we decided to walk to dinner after leaving the store. I wore my black Burberry coat with a removable lining. Technically a raincoat, this item became the only coat I could wrap around my burgeoning belly.

The sidewalks were jammed with people hurrying to leave work and get home. Adam grabbed my hand as we walked to steer me through the crowds, primarily to ensure I didn't fall over. With only about six weeks until my due date, I'd become balance challenged.

"Before I get home and dive into the candy, let's find a place to eat dinner because, shockingly, I'm hungry," I said.

We walked along Madison Avenue in search of food. Each restaurant we passed displayed a menu out front, and we paused to glance at several.

"Let's try this Italian restaurant," Adam said.

We entered the small building sandwiched between two high-end clothing boutiques. We didn't read the menu out front because the most glorious aroma filled the street as we walked up.

"Absolutely," I said. "If it smells this good, I can only imagine how fabulous the food will taste."

"Welcome to Nello. Have you joined us before?" the waiter asked.

"No," Adam said. "But everything looks and smells delicious."

After we sat at our table, I looked at the menu.

"Uh, Adam, I think the cheapest entrée is fifty dollars," I said.

"It's okay. You're hungry."

I loved Adam. He officially understood the feed-on-demand directive for the eight-month-pregnant wife.

I ordered a simple eighty-five-dollar pasta dish with tomato sauce. Although we'd have to pay for this meal out of our soon-to-be-born baby's college fund, this meal ranked as one of the best plates of pasta I'd ever eaten. I practically licked my plate.

"I hope everything was to your liking," the waiter said as he brought our bill.

"Yes, we thoroughly enjoyed everything," Adam said.

"Who knew my Jelly Belly craving would turn into one of the most expensive meals we'd ever eat," I said.

. . .

With Halloween in the air, while I was busy working on client projects and media campaigns at Vollmer Public Relations, the real work focused on what costume to wear at the annual office contest. This event was a big deal for the firm. One year, my coworker Christie and I went as Pink Ladies. We donned pink beehive wigs, rolled-up jeans, oversized white button-downs, and cat-eye glasses. Another year, my coworker Ashley and I went as "trailer trash" and wore tacky house-coats, slippers, and curlers.

With my due date one month away, I dressed as a pregnant bride. Despite all the maternity clothes I bought from Target and the fancy shop, nothing fit at this point in my pregnancy. Therefore, I wore whatever dress I could pull over my baby bump and threw on my wedding veil.

Vollmer operated in four locations—Houston, Dallas, Austin, and New York—and we all participated in our Halloween traditions. Each office celebrated with decorations, food, treats, costumes, and fun. To support each location, one executive from Houston, our corporate headquarters, traveled to a different office to join the fun.

Vollmer's CFO, Duane, traveled to New York to represent the executive team.

"What is your costume?" I asked him.

"I'm dressed like a CFO," he dryly replied.

"That's a typical money guy response," I said.

As we sat around the conference table feasting on lunch and Halloween treats (candy corn and Jelly Bellies for me), Duane, a father of two, talked to me about my upcoming delivery.

"When is your due date?" he asked.

"November twenty-third," I told him.

Then he pulled up the Farmer's Almanac on his computer.

"Hmm, you realize you'll probably have the baby a few days later," he said.

"Why do you say that?" I asked.

"Because according to the Farmer's Almanac, there's a full moon on November twenty-fourth, and it's said that women tend to go into labor during a full moon," he explained.

"That's just a myth," I said.

But I secretly wondered if he were right.

. . .

I continued working out with my trainer, Jenny, until the week before my due date. I looked like a hippopotamus walking through the gym. My appearance frightened people exercising around me. While working out with Jenny one afternoon, I saw my hairdresser, Eliut, who hailed from Puerto Rico.

"Judy, shoulda you be up there? What if your water breaks?" he asked in his accented English when he saw me hanging from the bars doing assisted pull-ups.

"She's a rock star!" Jenny said. "And she'll be fine. We're trying to move things along."

I may have looked ridiculous, but I had never felt stronger, physically or mentally.

And it's a good thing I had my strength. The night my water broke was a full moon and every labor and delivery room was occupied. I experienced twenty long hours of unsuccessful labor that resulted in an unplanned C-section. I guess Duane was right about the full moon, after all.

On the Sunday after Thanksgiving, at age forty-three, I gave birth to a beautiful, healthy baby boy named Jack. The adrenaline rush I experienced after delivering him invigorated me, making me believe I could conquer the world. And my pregnancy journey turned out to be as typical as you'd expect it to be if I had been in my twenties or thirties.

Eventually, my euphoric bubble burst, and sheer exhaustion and sleep deprivation took over my body. I felt every bit of a forty-plus mother. But even during those delirious first days of motherhood, I kept my eye on the prize. I reminded myself that age is only a number. But then I wondered why my number had to be so big.

Having It All

HOLLYWOOD PAINTS CHILDBIRTH as a glamorous event. The minute the baby comes out of the mother, it is placed on her chest for the first time, allowing the bonding to commence. Then, the baby is quickly whisked away to be cleaned up. The mother returns to her room, where a glam squad awaits to make her Instagram-worthy and ready to pose for a full spread in *People* magazine.

At least this is how I assumed it worked for new mothers like J.Lo. Soon after giving birth to twins, she appeared on the cover of *People*, posing like she hadn't broken a sweat throughout the whole birthing process and instantly began sleeping through the night. Why did she look so beautiful when I looked like a monster? And I only had one kid, not two.

Then there's the royal family. I never understood why Lady Di and, later, Princess Catherine were practically shoved outside the hospital hours after delivering their children to meet with their loyal subjects. And they looked so beautiful.

I could barely walk after my son arrived, much less stand upright in regular shoes. These ladies are like superheroes, holding their newborns while wearing heels and tiaras, waving to a gawking crowd eager to catch a glimpse of royalty.

None of this happened for me.

My reward for more than twenty hours of labor and an unplanned C-section was swollen ankles and bags under my eyes that looked like I packed them for an extended vacation. I learned that the swelling I experienced, known as edema, happens to some women after a C-section. Swelling can occur in the face, ankles, hands, and feet.

"Look at my ankles! I'm the Elephant Man," I cried to Adam. "The only shoes I can wear are my Uggs, which are too tight."

I called my doctor to see if he could help me.

"I'm swollen all over! Please tell me there's a water pill I can take to eliminate swelling," I cried to my doctor.

"You just need to get plenty of rest and stay off your feet," he instructed.

The doctor had forgotten about the baby he had delivered a few days before and that staying off my feet and getting rest wasn't on my new mom's agenda. I couldn't help but think my forty-something body had failed me and might have bounced back quicker had I been younger. I couldn't remember any of my friends suffering in this same way, so I assumed my advanced age was the culprit. Of course, I had no scientific research to confirm this assumption. I only had my gut, which was also swollen.

• • •

Maternity leave is a coveted time for new mothers to heal from childbirth, bond with their new babies, catch up on TV shows and movies, and get much-needed rest. Depending on the company you work for, time off for maternity leave can vary.

According to babycenter.com, the average time off for working women in the United States is ten weeks. Since the Family & Medical Leave Act was enacted, most women take off at least three months, some an entire year. This leave can be either paid or unpaid, or a combination of both.

The maternity leave policy for my company, which was small and family-owned, gave me two weeks plus any sick/personal/vacation days I hadn't used during the year. The official start of my leave began during the Thanksgiving holiday weekend. Because I hadn't used all my time off before Jack's birth, I stretched my leave to six weeks, returning to work in mid-January.

Once I brought Jack home, our new nanny, Christina, came to the apartment daily to get us into a routine and allow me time to sleep and heal. At least that became the goal. She'd arrive at 8:30 a.m. to feed, change, and play with Jack. We'd spend the mornings putting Jack in all the clothes he'd received from family and friends, turning him into a baby model. He looked cuter and cuter in each outfit. I also photographed and videotaped his every move.

"He's ready to be the next face of Baby Gap!" I told Christina. "Maybe I can retire."

Christina also organized and cleaned Jack's room and did his laundry. After she put him down for his afternoon nap, she went home.

"I may get very used to you," I jokingly told Christina.

So this is how J.Lo did it, times two.

While most of my maternity leave was spent bonding with Jack and planning his future supermodeling career, my mind never strayed far from client work. Toward the end of my six-week sabbatical, I spent more and more time on the phone and answering work emails.

"Judy, you need to rest and regain your strength, not be on email. You'll be back at work soon enough," Christina told me.

She was right, but I needed to pay attention to my clients and the office. The last thing I wanted was to return to a mound of work. The six weeks flew by, and looking back, I realized I should have listened to Christina. For the first time, I wondered what my life would look like if I were only a mom.

. . .

While on maternity leave, I frequently pushed Jack in his stroller around our Upper West Side neighborhood. Since it was wintertime, I often dipped into several stores and restaurants seeking warmth.

"What a precious baby," the salesperson at the Godiva store said. "Please come in from the cold and have a free piece of chocolate."

"Thank you, you're too kind," I replied.

Never one to pass on free chocolate, I obliged. And I went back several more times before returning to work, ensuring a different salesperson worked that day. Shortly afterward, the Godiva store closed. I prayed its shuttering had nothing to do with all the free samples given to me. But still, it's incredible how a cute newborn can draw such positive attention from others. And I took full advantage.

In January, my maternity leave days were dwindling. The temperatures outside became colder, and Jack and I barely left the apartment. The four walls were closing in on me.

"I need to get out of this apartment. I need a change of scenery," I cried to Adam over the phone while he was at the office.

"Okay, I'll come home, and we can drive to the Westchester," he said.

The Westchester, a local shopping mall about half hour from the city, housed every store in Manhattan, like Macy's and Williams-Sonoma, as well as kid-friendly restaurants like Cheesecake Factory and P.F. Changs. It became the perfect respite from my apartment and a go-to outing for us almost every weekend.

Adam and I timed our visits to the mall around dinnertime. Our routine included window-shopping as we pushed Jack in the stroller. Then we'd eat dinner at one of the restaurants while Jack snoozed in his infant carrier. But the best part of our shopping mall adventures was being able to sit, feed Jack his bottle, and people-watch. And, of course, visit the Godiva store.

"How sad that the highlight of my week is bringing Jack to a mall?" I said to Adam. "But when you think about it, every imaginable convenience is under one roof. We should move in."

Another baby-friendly place I spent time hibernating in during my maternity leave was Old John's Luncheonette, the diner across the street from our apartment.

The owner, Manny, his sons Sammy and Freddie, along with the friendly waitstaff, Cathy, Manuel, Clarence, Leo, and others, were kind to Adam and me and always treated us like family. Their special attention to us may have been because we treated their diner as our kitchen and ordered food practically every night. But after Jack's birth, the attention fell on him.

"Hello! Come in and sit right here," Manny said. "I'll make space for the little prince."

Jack practically grew up at the diner. Years later, when he got a little older, he sat at the counter with Manuel and others, charming them with his fun personality and thirst for knowledge, leaving Adam and me alone to enjoy our meal.

"Do I need to pay you by the hour?" I asked Manuel. "You're the best babysitter on the Upper West Side."

. . .

When my maternity leave ended, and it was time to return to work, I began questioning everything: Did I like being a stay-at-home mom? Could I put my career on hold for ten years and return to work once Jack was a little older? If I did, I'd be fifty-three when I returned to the workforce. Who'd even hire me?

And then my thoughts turned to my job. I was at the top of a career I had spent years building. I often wondered whether my work would suffer when I became a mother. And then I'd think, *Will I sacrifice being a good mom by focusing on my career?*

The thought of pausing or leaving the workforce confused me. I began working at age fifteen. How could I not work? Until my son's arrival, my career defined everything about me. I could think of nothing else. It's astonishing how the sentiment changes once you have a child.

I used to stand at the bus stop or on the subway platform on my way to work and judge women pushing babies in strollers. What did these women do all day?

Then I became one of these people. I finally realized how the job of motherhood is sometimes more complex than sitting in a corner office.

Like many career-focused women, working is in my fabric. Having a child was a bonus. I couldn't help it. I looked at my mother as a role model. She had a career in teaching and raised a great family. Her mom worked and raised a great family too. I'm sure her mom also worked and raised a great family. You do what you know.

When I first told people I was pregnant, they didn't say things like "Oh, are you going to quit working?" or "I'm sure you're going to slow down." Instead, I got "Well, this is going to be your *only* child, right?" and "I can't imagine *you* not working."

While I wasn't surprised by these comments (my coworkers and friends knew how career driven I was), they did make me question my reputation. Most of my friends returned to work after having their children, but they were much younger than I was when their babies were born. I was flying blind with my thoughts about potentially leaving my job and staying home to raise Jack. I found myself questioning my future. How could I leave my new baby with a stranger to raise, especially when I waited so long for him to arrive?

I've always found the phrase "you can have it all" so cliché when talking about a woman having a career and a family. I mean, would you settle for anything less than having it all? Not likely. What does having it all mean, anyway? And why couldn't "have it all" pertain to only being a wife and mother? I had no idea if this concept could be true, but I became determined to figure it out.

I ultimately returned to the office and got into a routine, leaving me to believe I could do this working mom thing. I could have it all. And while I often wondered if I still wanted it all, I knew no matter where my life took me, having a child, even later in life, would be my greatest legacy.

I'm Not a Stand-Up Comedian

I'VE ALWAYS BEEN FASCINATED by stand-up comedians and marveled at how they draw in their audiences with wit and humor through perfectly timed jokes. When I was a kid, my parents allowed my sister and me to stay up late to watch Johnny Carson perform his monologue on *The Tonight Show*. On occasion, we also watched Dean Martin's *Celebrity Roast*, where a parade of comedy legends such as Don Rickles, Milton Berle, Buddy Hackett, and Phyllis Diller slung mud at each other all night.

Through the years, I've been fortunate to see some great performances live, including Robin Williams, Joan Rivers, Jerry Seinfeld, and Jay Leno. I even met bad boy Andrew Dice Clay while eating dinner with a coworker at the Carnegie Deli in New York City.

"Yo, why you girls sitting by yourself with no men to pay for your dinner?" he asked us.

"Is this your way of saying you'll buy us dinner?" I replied.

He must have approved of my quick retort because he picked up our check.

My appreciation of comedy and sarcasm comes from growing up with a father who relentlessly teased my mother, sister, and me. Like most comedians, his humor was never meant to be malicious. If anything, it taught me to lighten up and never take myself too seriously.

This thinking is my approach to parenting.

Because I grew up in a house full of laughter and practical jokes, I love making others laugh, but I'm not a stand-up comedian.

. . .

A few months after my maternity leave, my boss, Helen, sent me to a workshop at a comedy club in New York City. The workshop aimed to help PR professionals understand how to apply stand-up comedy tools and concepts to our daily work and business.

"A comedy club?" I questioned Helen. "I'm so tired. Do I need to go to a club tonight?"

"It won't be that bad," Helen said. "It's a comedy club, and you'll hear a presentation, possibly enjoy a stand-up routine, and enjoy a free meal with an open bar. What's so horrible about that?"

While everything she listed was on the program, the one thing she missed was that attendees would be performing a short stand-up routine. Oh great. I already felt guilty for leaving Jack and Adam for the night, and now I'd get to embarrass myself in front of a room full of strangers by giving a stand-up act. Could this night get any better?

The comedy club was located off West 42nd Street in the heart of Manhattan's Theater District, also known as Off-Broadway. The dark club smelled dank and musty. Most of the walls were mirrored, making the club appear more significant than its size. Autographed headshots of famous and not-so-famous comedians filled the non-mirrored walls, giving the sense that you were somewhere important.

The emcee for the evening gave us direction for creating our routines.

"Think about what irritates you or a real-life experience others can relate to," he instructed the room. "You have five minutes to create your routine before performing on stage."

"I think I need a drink," I said to myself, or so I thought.

The speaker looked at me and said, "You'll go first."

Writing a short stand-up routine was no laughing matter for anyone in the room. I heard people saying, "We're in PR; we're not funny!" "What can a bunch of PR people come up with to say that is funny, much less for one to two minutes?" "We write talking points, not comedy."

Still, the results were shockingly humorous.

Fortunately for me, I was a new mom and had a world of material in the form of parenthood. I slung back my drink and proceeded to get up in front of a room full of my peers, none of whom I knew. I performed a stand-up routine on something that irritated me the most: unsolicited parenting advice from total strangers.

I walked onto the stage, took a deep breath and a large gulp of my drink, and said, "The other day, with our newborn strapped into his Bugaboo stroller, surrounded by every conceivable baby tool to keep him happy (three binkies, two lovies, two bottles, and my iPhone), my husband and I ventured out to our local Whole Foods Market. As we waited in line to empty our wallets for one bag of groceries, the baby started crying. At first, it was a squeak, but it soon turned into blood-curdling, window-busting screams that if I had been a simple observant, I would have called Child Protective Services."

Looking out at the room, I decided I picked a good topic that others could relate to because everyone was bobbing their heads and laughing. The more they laughed, the more I shared.

"As I tried everything to calm him down, short of standing on my head and balancing the items in my cart on my feet, a woman standing behind us offered her unsolicited opinion about why my son was crying. 'Oh, somebody must be tired or maybe hungry,' she sang as if she were part of a Broadway musical. I kindly looked at her and replied, 'Yes, I am hungry and deliriously tired, but enough about me.'"

And the laughter continued. Loudly. Of course, I'll never know if the audience laughed with or at me.

While still standing on stage, the emcee said to me, "You've done this before, right? You didn't seem nervous and you completely controlled the room."

"That's because I'm a mother," I replied. "And if you don't laugh at yourself and all the silly mistakes you'll make along the way, you'll end up in the fetal position every night staring at the bottom of a pint of Häagen-Dazs."

While the room again erupted in laughter as I finished my stand-up routine, I couldn't help but feel sad recounting my story. Don't get me wrong; I loved the positive reinforcement of laughter and felt like Sally Field when she won her Oscar. They like me, they really like me!

But I remembered the guilt I felt standing in line at Whole Foods; it was no laughing matter. I quickly learned that motherhood was just another word for guilt. And if a stranger could see I had no idea how to comfort my baby, what must my baby think? Fortunately, my son was the only audience member whose opinion mattered.

No matter how much guilt I may have had with leaving Adam at home with Jack to attend the workshop or with motherhood in general, relaying the Whole Foods incident to a room full of strangers helped me see that laughter is one of the most significant releases of tension, especially concerning parenthood. This one night of comedy helped me quickly learn that the insecurities you feel being a parent are a universally shared experience.

I've always been someone who can laugh at myself and find comedy and sarcasm in anything. These ideals helped me overcome my shame when I believed I was parenting the wrong way and ruining my son. Little did I realize this feeling was only the beginning and probably wouldn't ever go away.

Walking Zombie Mommy

THE MORNING OF MY FIRST day back to work, I woke up feeling excitement, sheer panic, and worry. The roller coaster of emotions reminded me of when my parents used to drop me off at summer camp. I was excited to see my coworkers and finally have adult conversations that went beyond feeding and pooping schedules. I panicked because I didn't know what to wear. I was no longer pregnant, but my non-maternity clothes still didn't fit me. I'd have to wear the least tent-like frock that didn't have spit up on the shoulder. I worried about leaving Jack with a stranger, even though I'd spent the last month with Christina and fully trusted her.

"I can't do this. How can I leave Jack?" I cried to Adam.

I had officially joined the legions of new mothers around the globe who muttered these exact words.

"It's going to be okay. You can do this," he assured me.

Easy for him to say.

When Adam returned to work after Jack was born, he'd spent even less time bonding and getting to know his new son than I had. He walked out the front door every morning, knowing I could handle it all. He wasn't attached to this little human in the same way I was.

Regardless of job demands and obligations, or how successful you become, there's something about saying goodbye to the tiny human who is now your sole responsibility. I began questioning my role.

Could I be a working mom without failing the motherhood part? Were these feelings a precursor of more thoughts to come? Would I be resentful? Would Jack hate me?

When I arrived at the office, my coworkers greeted me with hugs and smiles. Because ours was an office full of women, instead of getting straight to work, we all sat on the comfy sofa and oversized chairs in the reception area and passed around photos of Jack I'd happened to throw in my purse. Looking through the pictures and talking about Jack nonstop made me miss him slightly less than I initially expected. But once we returned to our individual offices to finally get the day started, I called Christina to check in.

"How's it going?" I asked her when she answered the phone. "I miss him."

"I know you do, but he's fine. You'll see him in a few hours."

"And I'm so tired," I whined.

No one tells you that if you're lucky enough to have a child in your forties, that's the easy part. Raising the child past midlife is what they should be warning you about. There's a reason women have babies in their twenties and thirties … they're younger! When you have a child in your forties, you've spent the prior two decades concentrating on life's most important thing: yourself. And you're used to getting at least eight hours of beauty sleep each night.

Also, when you're younger, and your skin has more elasticity, you can slap on a bunch of eye concealer, drink four to five cups of coffee, and you're ready to face the day. These hacks don't work for older moms with maturing skin. There's not enough concealer manufactured to hide the permanent dark circles and crevices that have formed underneath our tired eyes. I now needed spackle paste.

Making matters worse, Jack was a lousy sleeper from the time he was born, except when he was with the nanny. It was as if he didn't want to miss anything and cried and cried every night, refusing to go to sleep. Since he wasn't sleeping, Adam and I weren't sleeping, and we were often crankier than he was the next day. Fast-forward to today, and my sleep clock has never returned to normal.

"How many hours of sleep are you getting with the new little one?" many strangers asked when I returned to work. While I realized this question was only meant as small talk, I tended to take its meaning as "You look like crap and like you haven't slept in days." Clearly, I needed better spackle paste.

So, what is a sleep-deprived parent to do?

Honestly, I don't remember sleeping much during Jack's first year. But your body adapts, and muscle memory sets in, making you feel like a robot. About halfway through my first day back to work, my stomach started growling. I had gotten used to the feed-on-demand concept, including for myself.

"I'm going to grab a salad. I'll be right back," I told my coworkers.

I went to Metro Café, the restaurant at the foot of my office building. I'd frequented this restaurant for many years. After standing in line to select my salad toppings, I grabbed a drink and paid the cashier. At least, that's what I thought I did.

"Judy, are you okay?" asked the concierge of my building. "You look like you need to sit down."

"Where did this salad come from?" I asked him, looking at the bowl in my hands. "And why isn't it in a bag?"

I couldn't understand why I was standing in the middle of my building's lobby, holding a salad bowl with a drink in my other hand. And then it dawned on me.

"Oh my gosh! I walked out of the café without paying!"

I quickly ran back inside the restaurant and went up to the cashier.

"I'm so sorry," I said. "I walked out and forgot to pay you."

"We were wondering when you'd be back," she said, laughing. "We called your name as you walked out. We understand how tired you are with a new baby, so we decided to give you a few minutes since we knew you'd come back."

Being a regular at the café had its privileges. Any other restaurant I walked out of without paying almost certainly would have landed me in jail.

The first day back at work felt like the longest day of my life. This probably had to do with how often I sat at my desk wondering what Christina and Jack were doing. But I felt confident Jack was in great hands with Christina. I only called home three times, which I thought was reasonable.

"It's me again," I told Christina when I called after lunch. "How's my little man?"

"He's still good," she said.

I could feel her smile through the phone.

I'd never been a clock-watcher but on my first day back at work, that's all I did. At 5:30 p.m., I gathered my belongings and hurried to the subway. I couldn't wait to get home.

Christina and I developed a routine. I'd come home from the office every night at about 6:00, she'd tell me about Jack's day and anything new that had happened while I was away, and then she'd leave and return the following day at 8:00 a.m., allowing me enough time to get to my job by 8:30.

About three months after I'd returned to work, our routine became disrupted one night when Christina quickly left the apartment without any conversation about her and Jack's day.

"I'll see you tomorrow morning," she said as she ran out the door.

"Okay," I replied. "Is everything all right?"

I don't think she heard me because she jumped on the elevator the minute it stopped on our floor. While I thought our exchange felt odd, I didn't think much of it until I saw a gigantic purple welt in the middle of Jack's forehead.

"Oh, honey, does this hurt?" I asked Jack.

Of course, he couldn't talk yet, so I'm not sure what I expected him to say to me. I quickly got an ice pack to apply to Jack's forehead. Adam entered the door as I sat on the couch, cradling Jack.

"What happened, and what are you doing?" he asked me as he saw the ice pack.

"There's a big purple welt on Jack's forehead, and it's getting darker," I told him. "I don't know what happened because Christina practically ran out of the apartment when I got home."

At about the same time, the phone rang, and Christina's husband was on the line.

"Christina needs to speak to Judy to apologize," he told Adam.

With a puzzled look on his face, Adam handed me the phone.

"It's Christina," he said. "She wants to apologize to you."

I looked at Adam with concern and took the phone.

"Christina, are you okay?" I asked her.

Her sobs were so loud I could barely understand a word she said.

"I'm so sorry," I finally heard her say through loud gasps of air.

My heart started racing.

"I was playing with Jack on the floor, and the remote control fell off the table and banged him on his forehead. I panicked and didn't know what to do."

I calmed down once I realized what had happened and knew Jack would be okay.

"Oh my gosh, don't be so upset over this accident. Frankly, I'm surprised this hasn't happened to me yet. But promise me you'll always tell me if something like this happens again. I won't be mad unless you do something intentionally, which I know you wouldn't."

When it came to Christina, I felt blessed and relieved. I genuinely believed the nanny gods were with me when it came to finding her. Her calm, sweet nature complimented my anxiousness and helped quash my neurotic feelings of leaving Jack every day. Fortunately, because I spent so much of my maternity leave with her, we got to know each other well. I truly trusted that she would have Jack's best interest in mind with everything she did for him.

While it's hard to imagine a remote control could cause such a large welt on a baby's forehead, this wasn't any remote control. It looked like a minicomputer that could control a NASA rocket. It weighed about two pounds. I hated it with every fiber of my being. You needed a degree from MIT to use it, and I could never get it to turn on the TV or change the channel.

"That's it!" I yelled. "We are throwing this ridiculous contraption away for good."

We only had this remote control because my father had one too. On one of my parents' many flights, my father came across this behemoth in an airline magazine. And because he bought one, he wanted Adam to have one as well. I couldn't believe it took Jack's forehead getting smashed to finally convince us to throw away the brick for good.

I knew this would be the first of many boo-boos and oopsies for Jack. And I'd probably miss a lot of them. Was I better off outsourcing his care to Christina? As ridiculous as this sounded, I was jealous that Christina had been there to comfort Jack when that stupid remote control fell on his head. Did this mean he didn't need me? As he got older, would he start crying for Christina when he fell and skinned his knee? Was I missing out?

Pity party, table for one!

Every new mom suffers from insecure thoughts and feelings about being a good or at least "good enough" mother, and I'm no different. The truth: I was conflicted about continuing the career I'd spent years building. Did I want to stay home with Jack? I didn't know the answer, and honestly, there's no right or wrong answer. Instead, at least for this one evening, I decided to drink a big glass of wine and greet Christina with a smile the following day when she walked through the front door for another fun-filled day with Jack.

Who Stays Home with the Baby?

I MOVED TO NEW YORK CITY as a single woman in my late thirties. My parents lived in Florida and my close relatives and friends lived in Texas, so I didn't have people nearby to help in times of emergency. While I mostly managed fine on my own, I didn't have the luxury of dropping Jack at his grandparents' house for the night, weekend, or month when I felt overwhelmed or wanted to be with Adam or my girlfriends. I relied heavily on nannies and babysitters and found myself coordinating around their schedules rather than mine.

I frequently traveled to Texas for my job at the public relations agency. Not having a support system in proximity to help me with Jack became challenging. When Jack was two months old, I took my first business trip to Texas to work in our Houston office. Pre-Jack, I barely planned for these trips. I'd pack my carry-on bag, grab my laptop, and fly to my destination. Coordinating a business trip with a newborn is challenging. I spent more time preparing Jack's paint-by-number and day-by-day activities than I did for my trip. But once I arrived in Houston, I treated the time away like a vacation.

My cousin, Kay, invited me to stay with her while I was in Houston, but I told her that I wanted some time to myself. I wanted to rest.

"Don't stay in a hotel," Kay said. "You can stay with us."

"It's not that I don't want to spend time with you," I told her. "I want to be by myself."

"You had to fly to Houston to get some rest?" she asked me.

"Yes, that is precisely why I flew to Houston and what I will do," I said.

After a busy day at the office, my coworkers wanted to go out to dinner.

"Thank you for the invitation," I told them. "But I have important plans for the evening."

After politely turning down the dinner invite, I checked into my hotel room, turned the AC on low, ordered room service, and watched a movie on pay-per-view. I was in heaven. I missed Jack and Adam, but there's nothing like a good night of sleep to recharge a tired mom's battery.

· · ·

When Jack was almost four months old, I had to attend more client meetings in Houston. I decided to fly to Florida and drop Jack with my parents. A win-win for everybody.

"I have to fly back to Houston, and instead of leaving Jack in New York, can I drop him off at your house and come back for the weekend after my meetings?" I asked my mother.

"Like you have to ask," she said. "Yes, you can drop Jack off with us, but don't rush back to get him."

My mother would keep Jack for months if I'd let her. And I would have been happy to oblige, but after a few days in Houston, I started missing Jack, not the interrupted sleep, but his cute little face.

A few months later, back in New York, my phone rang as I was dressing for work. It was Christina, Jack's nanny. She was sick and not coming to work. I hung up the phone and went into crisis mode.

"I have a client meeting today, and I can't stay home with Jack," I told Adam. Zoom didn't exist in 2008.

"I'm also super busy at work," he replied.

I panicked. But I knew my hysteria wouldn't fix the problem. With no available babysitters, especially at 7:00 a.m., and no early morning flights to Florida to drop off Jack at my parents' house, I had no choice but to take him to the office with me. Fortunately, being the office's general manager, I had leeway and the ability to make this decision. Being an older mom did have its advantages in times like this.

"Okay, let's pack Jack's stuff, and I'll bring him to my office," I said. "With a room full of women, one of them will watch him while I'm on my conference call."

I stuffed the diaper bag full of bottles, binkies, diapers, toys, food, and a few changes of clothes and threw the Pack 'n Play into the back of the car. Before we got to the office, I called my coworker, Katelyn, a former nanny, and one of the most nurturing women I knew, to meet me in the lobby. When Adam pulled up in front of my building, she was there with a bright, cheery smile, instantly calming my nerves.

"Thank you for meeting me to haul all Jack's stuff upstairs," I said. "I hope he's not a total distraction to everyone today."

"Are you kidding me," Katelyn said. "We're all so excited to play with him. I hope we get some work done."

When we got upstairs, my coworkers helped me set up the Pack 'n Play in one of the empty offices. Unfortunately, Jack fell asleep in the car on the way to the office, so he was wide awake and in no mood to take his morning nap.

The office was compact, with a small front reception area when one entered the door. Because of the limited space, we only had a loveseat and two comfy high-back chairs for people to sit on. Along the wall was a conference room and four windowed offices overlooking Madison Avenue, more precisely, into the windows of workers across the street. Cubicles filled the open area in the middle, and a small kitchenette and mechanical room completed the space in the back.

I spread Jack's blanket on the floor in the reception area, and all the girls gathered around to play with him.

"Okay, who will help me by watching Jack during my conference call today?" I asked. "This doesn't mean you don't have to get your work done, but I'll take any and all help."

While I needed everyone's help throughout the day, I was their boss, and client work took precedence, no matter how cute Jack appeared. Like attorneys and accountants, public relations firms make money by the hour. I could only imagine explaining to a client why we billed time for "playtime with Jack."

"We'll take shifts," Katelyn said. "You won't even know he's here."

"Until he starts crying," I said.

I brought Jack into my office and kept him on my lap while I prepared for my conference call. Knowing Katelyn and the others could occupy Jack while I was on the phone lowered my stress level for the remainder of the day.

Each time my phone rang, Katelyn or someone else would come to take Jack from me so he wouldn't blow my cover. I was totally paranoid, worrying he'd start screaming if I was on the phone with a client or, worse, my boss. I eventually told my boss, Helen, that Jack was in the office.

"I get it," she told me. "Do you know how often I had to bring my girls to the office?"

"Thank you," I said. "I promise this won't become a habit."

But it got me thinking about a scenario where I could simultaneously work from home and raise Jack. Of course, I wouldn't have

Katelyn and the others around to help me, so I quickly shelved the idea.

Around noon, we all gathered in the conference room for lunch, as we often did, and I fed Jack. After lunch, I tried to put him down for his nap. He wanted nothing to do with this plan.

"Please, honey, please stop crying and go down for your nap," I pleaded.

"Do you want me to try?" Katelyn asked. "You need to get ready for your call."

"Yes, thank you," I said. "This is why I have a nanny. I have no idea how to do this."

Katelyn got Jack to sleep in what felt like five minutes.

"He probably felt your stress," she kindly said. "Babies sense everything."

"Given how my day started, Jack must have felt a lot of panic from the minute he woke up," I said.

Jack spent the day sleeping, eating, laughing, crying, crawling around the floor, putting everything in his mouth, and being passed around by all the girls. He charmed each of them with his cute smile and big blue eyes. But as successful as this little adventure was, I wanted to avoid repeating it anytime soon.

"I survived my first take-your-child-to-work day," I told Adam on the way home. "Next time, you take him to your office."

Are You in Menopause?

ONE BEAUTIFUL FALL NIGHT, Adam and I decided to hire a baby-sitter and enjoy the unseasonably warm temperatures. We went to a local wine bar across the street from our apartment. We frequented this place and knew the owners well.

"What do you want to drink?" Adam asked.

"I'm going to have club soda with a lemon," I told him. "I'm still trying to get rid of this headache I've had for the past two days."

While I would have enjoyed a nice glass of wine, sitting outside and taking in the city was equally pleasurable.

"Nice to see you both," Mark, the wine bar owner, said as he greeted us. "Judy, why aren't you drinking tonight? Are you pregnant? You know it's time to finally give your son a sibling."

This question and comment from family and friends crossed the line, let alone from a relative stranger. And while I'm sure Mark was making small talk and probably joking, his comment made me cringe. I could have told him about my headache. Instead, I was inclined to give further explanation and justification.

"I think I'm too old and tired to have another child," I said.

"You're not that old," he replied.

"Yes, I am," I said. "I just had a milestone birthday, the big five-oh."

He stared at me like a light bulb popped on inside his head.

"Oh, then again, maybe you can *no longer* have a child. My wife is about your age and just went into menopause."

In less than five minutes, the conversation went from asking why I wasn't drinking wine to wondering whether I was pregnant to suggesting I was in menopause. I thought this was a wine bar, not *Cheers*.

. . .

The gabfest with our local bar owner got me thinking about other awkward questions some people feel are appropriate to ask, whether they know you well or not. I started getting questions about having another child from family and strangers after Jack's first birthday, and while I mostly answered them directly, some of my responses were in my head.

"When will you start trying for a little brother or sister for your son?"

Am I mistaken, or did you just ask if I am having sex? Clearly, this question is very personal and shouldn't be asked by close family, friends, or a random person standing in the checkout aisle of the grocery store.

"Will you get your child a puppy instead?"

Implying that a puppy is a substitute for a baby brother or sister is ridiculous. While most children would love to have a little sibling(s) to torment, if a couple decides (or has no choice) to stop at one, they shouldn't be made to feel a family pet will fill an empty place at the dinner table. Although, I've always wanted a dog.

"You're so lucky you only have one child. I'm so tired all the time with two."

Parenting is exhausting whether you have one, two, or ten children. It's not a contest of who is more overwhelmed, does more laundry, or gets the least amount of sleep. Stop bragging about how inept you are at being a parent. After all, you decided to have more than one, right?

"Your house must be so quiet with just one child."

I'm sure "quiet" doesn't describe any home with children. Yes, the decibel level in a house full of kids is higher than in a house of one, but that doesn't mean it's like being in a library.

"How do you teach your child to share?"

Hopefully the same way you teach your children to share. Just because I have only one child doesn't mean they rule the roost and aren't taught manners.

"My friend thought she just wanted one child, and when she had another, she said her life was finally complete."

And I'm sure your friend's therapist is working overtime helping her through her other issues.

The truth is, I would have loved to give Jack a sibling. It wasn't in the cards for Adam and me. And not for lack of trying. After suffering three miscarriages, I didn't believe having a child was in my future. By the time Jack was born, I was forty-three and Adam was forty-five. Most people in their forties buy fancy sports cars, travel the world, or get plastic surgery to deal with a midlife crisis. I had a baby. And maybe I did some of these other things too.

Of course, it's not only total strangers questioning your life choices. Sometimes, girlfriends who have been in your life since high school pass judgment. One summer while visiting her son, Michael, in New York City, Annette, my lifelong friend from Houston, came with me to get Jack from the camp bus. As we waited for the bus to drive up, she turned to me and said, "I can't believe you're fifty and you have a child in summer camp. What were you thinking?"

I understood Annette's question wasn't meant to be unkind or hurtful. I'd asked myself this question many times before. But while so many answers swirled in my head of how to respond to her, I simply said, "This is how my life is supposed to be, and I wouldn't change a thing."

When you have a child in your forties, you're constantly doing the math in your head of how old you'll be when your child starts school and when they graduate from high school. You wonder if you'll be able to see them get married and give you grandchildren. Having another child meant I'd be even older for these milestones.

· · ·

Adam and I sat at our table that glorious fall evening, taking in all the sights and sounds of New York City. Mark, the wine bar owner, came up to our table to refill our water glasses. Fortunately, this time, he refrained from speaking. As we sat listening to the sirens and horns fill the night air, and watching all the people scurrying along the sidewalk, I couldn't help but think how content I felt about my life. I lived in one of the most vibrant cities in the country, was married to a wonderful man who put up with all my quirks and sarcasm, and together we had a beautiful son who brought us so much joy, along with many gray-hair-inducing antics.

So what if I stopped after one child? I felt blessed to have Jack and beyond scared to try again. I felt anxious enough about Jack being an only child. The last thing I needed was a wine bar owner making me feel worse about my decision and asking me if I was going through menopause.

I Love New York

Space – The Final Frontier

LIVING IN NEW YORK CITY isn't for the faint of heart. Between small apartments, cramped closets, crowded streets, never-ending noise, and the astronomical cost of living, you're constantly asking yourself why you live here. For me, I couldn't imagine living anywhere else. Sure, I grew up in Texas with wide open spaces. Moving to Manhattan with no open space and everything vertical was a big shock. But I loved it.

While Adam and I were still dating, we'd often discuss our future.

"If you could choose between staying in New York City and owning an apartment versus moving out of the city and having a child, which would you pick?" Adam asked.

"I'd choose living in the city and having a child," I said. "I want it all."

After Adam and I married, the decision of whether to stay in the city or move out became a regular conversation. Would we be happier in the 'burbs? What would our life be like away from the city and its conveniences? And really, what would we do with all that storage space in a house? Were we really throwing all our money away on rent when we could buy a big house for the same price? The decision to stay or go is mainly based on commuting, cost, and closet space.

Before I found out I was pregnant—for the fourth time—Adam and I decided to stay in New York City and search for a larger apartment. Regardless of whether a baby was in our future, we needed more room.

"We've got to find a place with an extra bedroom and more closets," I told Adam. "We're busting at the seams with all our crap."

Making matters worse, we'd rented a storage locker outside of the city to house even more of the belongings we didn't have room for in our apartment: extra furniture, pictures, CDs, boxes of old tax returns, rugs, large suitcases, and other things we no longer needed and hadn't seen or used in years.

Should we buy a house to store all this stuff? I often wondered.

The evening I found out I was pregnant, Adam and I had an appointment to see a new unit in our apartment building. We had been eyeing a larger unit for years, and one was finally available to rent.

After I left work and before I met up with Adam, I made a pit stop at home and took a pregnancy test. Something had felt off all day. I'd gotten familiar with how my body felt when I was pregnant, and in that moment, I felt pregnant. And the test confirmed it.

I left our apartment and took the elevator up to the thirty-fourth floor to meet Adam. He and one of the building supervisors, Sammy, were waiting for me.

"Here are the keys," Sammy said. "Drop them off at the desk when you're finished and take your time."

Since I'd lived in the building for five years, I'd become friendly with Sammy and many other workers. They felt like family, a bonus to apartment-living in Manhattan. Adam and I entered the sprawling three-bedroom, three-bath pad over-looking Central Park and Midtown Manhattan. While mesmerized by the amount of space, number of closets, and views this unit offered, extra space was the last thing on my mind at that moment.

"What do you think?" Adam asked me.

"It's great. Let's take it. I'm pregnant," I told him in rapid response.

Because the apartment was empty, my words vibrated off the walls. Adam stared at me as if he hadn't understood what I said.

"Did you hear me?" I asked.

"Yes," he said. "I guess we'll sign the new lease."

The streets of the Upper West Side were filled with kids, and plenty of babies lived in our building. Still, I wondered if we'd made the right decision to stay and not move to the 'burbs. I remembered my conversation with Adam years earlier when he asked me if I wanted an apartment in Manhattan or a baby. Of course, the new apartment also included more space. I didn't know what excited me more: a new baby or extra closets.

One month later, Adam and I moved from the twenty-third to the thirty-fourth floor. City apartment dwellers often prefer to move into a different unit within the same building to avoid the hassle of moving out of the building. This was the second time Adam and I had done this shift.

On the morning of the move, Adam stayed in the old apartment, working with the movers, while I waited in the new apartment for the cable guy. I left the front door open as I waited.

"Hello, are you my new neighbor?" a man from across the hall asked me.

"Yes, I'm Judy. We're moving up from the twenty-third floor," I told him.

"I'm Howard. Nice to meet you. Do you have any kids?" he asked.

"No," I said.

I wondered if he could tell I was pregnant.

"Are you planning on having kids?" he asked.

Okay, this is a personal question, but I'll answer it.

"Well, I'm not sure yet, Howard. Have you been talking to my mother or something?"

He laughed and explained that the former tenants had noisy kids and threw loud parties late into the night.

"Come in and let me show you my bedroom wall," he said.

I reluctantly followed him into his apartment. He showed me his bedroom, which shared a wall with our living room.

"I promise we're quiet," I told him.

I'd have to remember to keep quiet when in the living room or suffer Howard's wrath.

Wait until he finds out I'm pregnant.

As Adam and I unpacked our belongings and filled the closets, I couldn't help smiling at the thought that soon we'd have a third person living with us. I always loved the idea of raising a child in Manhattan because it looked so easy on television shows like *Family Affair*, *Diff'rent Strokes*, and *The Nanny*. Of course, those families lived in penthouses and townhomes with multiple massive living spaces, walk-in closets, eat-in kitchens, and separate dining rooms. And the children had full-time childcare, butlers, and drivers.

If only life could imitate art.

. . .

Several months later, before we brought Jack home from the hospital, I started thinking about how my neighbor Howard would react to seeing Jack and how he would handle a baby crying. His personal questioning of whether Adam and I would have children led me to believe he might not be thrilled to learn he'd soon have a new neighbor, especially one who would cry and be up at all hours of the night.

"I hope Jack's crying doesn't disturb Howard," I said to Adam. "He was very anxious wanting to know if we had kids or were planning to have any."

"He'll be okay, I'm sure," Adam said. "Besides, he's a father too."

A few days after we came home from the hospital, Howard knocked on our door.

"So, you *were* planning on having kids," he said with a laugh.

"Well, I *was* pregnant when you first asked," I said.

"I'm very happy for you both, and I must say, you are the quietest neighbors I've ever had. I bought a little something for the baby."

He gave Jack the most beautiful blanket. A kind and thoughtful gift.

"I hope you still feel the same way after a few nights of Jack crying," I said.

He laughed. I didn't.

Adventures in Finding a Nanny

THE IDEA OF LEAVING my new baby with a stranger freaked me out. Probably because I'd watched so many of those "nightmare nanny" movies on Lifetime. Also, I couldn't believe after I had waited so long to have a child, after all the losses and challenges, that I'd soon be leaving him with a total stranger. Was I irrational to do this?

I loved my career in public relations, and I was good at my job. The jury was still out on how well I'd thrive at my new job of motherhood. A few months before Jack was born, I started my nanny search by going online to find names of nanny agencies around the city. Then I randomly called each one for more information. This process reminded me of my move to New York and my experience with Rona, the apartment broker.

"Rona, how do you get paid?" I asked.

"I only get paid if I find you an apartment," she said. "And that fee is thirty percent of your rent."

"Rona, I only need you to find me an apartment, not move in with me," I said.

She didn't appreciate my humor.

Like apartment brokers, nanny agencies collect enormous fees. But who knew if you'd get a good, trustworthy nanny for your money?

Another popular way for many New York City parents to find good nannies included luring an existing caregiver away from another family by offering them more money. If you read *The Nanny Diaries*, you understand this concept.

"Maybe I'll hang out in Central Park at the playground and poach a nanny," I told Adam. Although I'd be furious if someone did that to us.

I decided to change course and turn to nanny websites. I'd found my husband through an online dating site, so I'd find a good person to take care of my child. Right?

Nanny websites, while obscure in 2007, did exist and included an exhaustive questionnaire for the nanny and the family.

"I think I've solved the problem of illegal immigration," I told Adam. "If you're a potential nanny and want to be on this site, the first question is if you are legally allowed to work in the US. Do you know how many have answered that question no?"

I decided nanny websites were a Department of Homeland Security treasure trove.

After filling out the parameters of what we wanted in a potential nanny (much like finding the perfect husband), including age, experience, location, and education, I found a young woman I thought might be a good fit for us.

"She looks good," I told Adam. "She has experience with infants, an early childhood education background, and is legally allowed to work in the US. Let's contact her."

This woman lived in Brooklyn, and we decided to meet at a Starbucks near Columbus Circle, a short walk from our apartment and close to her subway station. Adam and I arrived a few minutes early to get a table. About forty minutes past the scheduled meeting time, I told Adam to forget it. We'd been stood up. This process felt eerily like dating.

Adam's phone rang as we were walking out of the coffee shop.

"I'm so sorry, but I got on the wrong train, and now I'm lost, but I think I can meet you in about an hour," she said.

"No, thank you," Adam said.

I couldn't help thinking about the colossal bullet we just dodged. Imagine getting a call at work: Hello, I'm in Central Park with your baby, but I'm lost and can't find my way home.

Oh well, back to the drawing board.

The next candidate seemed to be a very qualified young woman who had worked at a local Jewish day school and recently left that job to get a master's degree in early childhood education. She was looking for a permanent nanny position. Adam and I liked what we saw on paper, at least. After our unsuccessful try at Starbucks with the previous candidate, we decided to conduct the meeting at our apartment.

"If I'm your nanny, I have to let you know I'll need all the Jewish holidays off, and I'll have to leave early every Friday for the Sabbath," she explained.

"That's not a problem, as we take off work for Rosh Hashanah and Yom Kippur, and we're happy to work with your schedule on Fridays," I told her.

"Oh, it wouldn't be just the high holidays," she said. "It would be every holiday on the calendar."

She rattled off several holidays including Tu Bishavt (birthday of trees) and Shavuot (week of feasting where you only eat dairy), and others I'd never heard of before. This would be approximately twenty-nine days off. Plus, leaving early every Friday and never working on Saturday. While we would never sit in judgment of anyone's religious practice (since we wouldn't want anyone to judge our beliefs), we decided to pass.

A broader search led us to Christina—a young, recently married, Vassar graduate.

Our first meeting with Christina occurred at Old John's, the diner across the street from our apartment, where the staff was like family.

Upon meeting Christina, I could tell she was a lovely, sweet-natured, calm woman who loved babies. Precisely what we hoped for in a nanny. Nothing seemed to rattle her nerves, including my anxiety.

"Why do you want to be a nanny?" I asked her. "This is my first child, and I'm a little nervous about hiring a nanny to essentially raise him while I work."

"I totally understand, but I want you to know I love babies," she assured me. "I originally went to school to become a pediatrician, but it was too much school. Being a nanny is very rewarding."

Christina's experience included a nanny position and several babysitting stints. Her calmness countered my nervousness, and I believed she would be great for our family.

"When can you start?" we asked her.

"I'm happy to begin once the baby is born and be available to you while you're still on maternity leave," she said. "That way, you can get your rest, and I can start getting the baby on a regular schedule."

"Uh, do you think you can get me on a regular schedule too?" I joked.

We ended our meeting by promising to follow up with her in a few days.

"What do you think?" I asked Adam when we got back to our apartment.

"I like her," he said. "She seems so calm, something we probably won't be."

"Am I crazy to leave our child with a total stranger?" I asked.

"You can't take him to work," Adam said.

"I know that, but how will I ever be able to leave him, especially with someone we barely know?" I cried.

I wasn't sure if my anxiety was about leaving our newborn with someone we barely knew, or if it centered on going back to work, or both. Regardless, I knew I had only two choices: hire Christina or quit my job.

A few days later, after a background and reference check, we called Christina with an offer, and she accepted.

"You'll be one of the first calls we make once the baby is born," we told her. "So be sure to keep your phone on."

. . .

After Christina agreed to be our nanny, it dawned on me that we hired a practical stranger to care for our baby. I realized Adam and I weren't the first new parents to do this, but it felt so strange. But we hired a caregiver for our child, not a pet sitter for our dog. We liked Christina a lot and felt comfortable knowing she'd be caring for Jack. The whole concept of paying someone to, in a sense, raise your child while you worked felt so foreign to me. I prayed my nerves would subside before the day arrived when I had to go back to work. I hoped I'd calm down and not make Christina feel uncomfortable.

As we hung up the phone, I turned to Adam and said, "I wonder if Christina is more nervous about caring for our new baby or dealing with me?"

The Thousand-Dollar Stroller

SELECTING A STROLLER for the streets of Manhattan is like buying a good mountain bike. Suspension and brakes are more important than portability and weight. If you're riding the trails of Moab, you want to avoid flying over the handlebars when going over rough terrain. I can say the same for the streets of New York City. Maneuvering around uneven sidewalks and pedestrians at every step, you want to ensure your baby is secure and doesn't go flying.

Enter the Bugaboo. The Rolls-Royce of strollers.

When Adam and I went stroller shopping for Jack, we wanted to guarantee it would be comfortable for him and us since we'd "drive" it around the city. The most popular stroller at the time was the Bugaboo, and you couldn't walk a block on the Upper West Side of Manhattan without seeing a baby being pushed in one. The engineering and design ranked well above other strollers, and the marketing of the Bugaboo was genius as well.

When you bought the Bugaboo, you only purchased the stroller. Anything else, like a storage basket, cup holder, or umbrella, came separately. One baby guide we read compared buying a Bugaboo stroller to a hotel mini bar since everything cost extra and was overpriced.

"Who pays over a thousand dollars for a stroller?" I asked Adam before we bought the Bugaboo. "Are we crazy?"

Adam, an expert with numbers, replied, "It's worth the investment if we only have to buy one stroller over Jack's lifetime of needing it."

He was right since most of my friends living outside New York City told me they went through multiple strollers. They had bought cheap strollers that could fold up like an umbrella and eventually fell apart—meaning they constantly had to replace them. Being older parents helped us rationalize that a thousand-dollar baby stroller was a good investment, like a luxury car, and not an impulse purchase.

. . .

Strolling a baby around the city was never a grab-and-go affair. Before leaving the apartment, you had to ensure you had enough toys, snacks, water, scooters, helmets, and money to make it through the day. And since the stroller weighed a lot without the extras, adding more crap meant adding more weight. Also, carrying the stroller was a full-blown workout: up and down stairs, to and from the subway, on and off the bus. All while balancing Jack on one hip.

Once you stuff the stroller full of necessities, you're tasked with pushing through the streets, fighting crowds of people, cars, taxis, bikers, and buses. And not every day is a Better Business Bureau brochure day with blue skies, low humidity, mild temperatures, and perfect hair.

"I'm definitely too old for this routine," I told Adam.

"That's why we work out," he replied.

"I can't wait for Jack to be out of the stroller and walking alone. I'm exhausted," I said.

As Jack got older, we shifted away from the Bugaboo. We started using a lighter weight stroller we bought that was easier to fold when traveling by bus, taxi, or airplane. But even though the stroller was lighter, Jack was getting heavier. But a bonus was pushing it and him around all day allowed me to skip my arm workout.

. . .

Then, the day finally arrived. Jack was four years old when I felt comfortable ditching the stroller and walking with him around the city, holding his hand. I wished I hadn't been in such a hurry.

Even though I felt Jack could handle moving around the city without a stroller, the jury was still out for me. Regardless, I didn't put either of the strollers away for good. Knowing your young child is securely strapped in while maneuvering around a busy city brings comfort.

One of our first outings sans stroller was to the local grocery. Food shopping in suburbia means you can put your child in the cart and push them around the market. This would be a luxury in New York City with its small stores and narrow aisles.

"Jack, hold my hand and don't let go," I told him as we walked around the Food Emporium, a local grocery store across the street from our apartment. "I just need to get a few things, and then we'll be done."

While scanning my items in the self-checkout lane, I dropped Jack's hand for a second to get my wallet. Once I had my credit card ready to put into the machine, I turned around to grab Jack's hand, and he was gone.

Frantically, I whipped around, calling his name.

"Jack, Jack, where are you?" I screamed.

People looked at me like I was talking to myself.

"Did you see the little boy standing right next to me?" I asked anyone who would listen to me. "He was just here, and now he's not."

As I stood in shock, with tears streaming down my face, people looked at me as if I were a mental case. But worse, no one claimed to have seen him. In that moment, I wished I could call Detectives Benson and Stabler from *Law & Order SVU* to help me find Jack.

"He was just here!" I screamed.

I ran around the checkout area where we'd stood, and something told me to look outside the store. Not thinking, I left my purse and wallet beside my groceries and ran out the door. I found Jack standing on the corner of Broadway and West 68th Street, crying and screaming, "Mommy! Mommy!"

"Jack!" I screamed. "Honey, I'm here."

I grabbed him into my arms, not wanting to let go until he turned sixteen.

He shook and cried harder.

"Why did you run away from me?" I asked as I wiped his tear-stained cheeks. "I was so scared because I couldn't find you. You know you're not supposed to run away from Mommy."

"I wanted to see what was outside," he said. "And then I didn't know where you were."

We had taught Jack all about "stranger danger" and the importance of never talking to people he didn't know. But his curiosity had gotten the better of him, so he'd walked outside.

Seeing my child standing on a busy street corner in Manhattan with a hoard of people bustling around shook me. Sure, I needed to cut the cord with Jack and the stroller, especially since it became harder and harder to push him as he got older. But clearly, we both needed more time to transition.

Fortunately, when we returned to the store, my purse and wallet were still next to the groceries. I paid, and we went home.

"What's wrong?" Esad, our doorman and a father to young twins, asked me as we entered our building. "You look like you've seen a ghost."

One of the great things about living in a high-rise apartment is that the staff become extended family. It's incredible how much they learn about you, your family, and your daily habits. Before I'd told anyone I was pregnant with Jack, for example, one of our doormen, Paul, figured it out. One morning he said congratulations and winked as I walked out the door. To this day, I have never understood how he figured it out.

I explained to Esad what had happened at the grocery store. He came around from his desk and crouched down to Jack's level.

"Jack, you can never run away from Mommy," he said. "That is very dangerous, and no one wants you to get hurt, okay?"

Jack appeared to listen intently. "Okay, I promise," he said.

With so little family around to help me with Jack, I loved being surrounded by such a kind, compassionate group of people to support me. And, at the very least, make sure Jack never snuck out of the building.

. . .

By the time Jack entered kindergarten, we were using the strollers less and less. We eventually gave them both away. But our investment was well worth the money we spent, especially since we didn't have to replace either of them in six-plus years. I'm confident I have never owned a car for as long.

While Jack was thrilled with his newfound independence, I was sad. As much as I complained about pushing Jack and all his belongings up and down hills, I recognized we'd reached the end of an era. My baby was growing up.

Jack's Harem

ABOUT TEN MONTHS after Christina, Jack's nanny, began working with us, she made an unexpected announcement.

"I've decided to go back to school and get another degree," she told us. "I'll continue working for you, but I'll need to reduce my days."

This put Adam and me in a strange place, as we worked full-time, five days a week. The thought of finding a new nanny overwhelmed me.

"I can't believe we have to return to the drawing board," I said to Adam.

After an exhaustive internet search, I found Desirée, a graduate of UCLA (Adam's alma mater). She had recently moved to New York from California and was still figuring out her plan. Fortunately, our timing fit perfectly with her non-existent plan.

Desirée was a godsend, and Jack loved her. She nannied for several children, including twins, while living in California. She only worked for us two days a week, but she'd often volunteer to come to our apartment on Saturday mornings, allowing us to sleep in or go to the gym.

"You're spoiling us," I'd often tell her.

Not surprisingly, two months into Christina's cutback schedule, she decided to become a full-time student. She hated to leave Jack, but she wanted to pursue her studies full-time. We told her we understood and encouraged her to follow her dreams.

If we hadn't found Desirée to fill in, I would have been stressed out and probably angry. Clearly, Christina had aspirations beyond nannying. I got it, though. That's the price we paid for hiring young college-educated women. They didn't want to make a career out of caring for other people's children. Even though Jack was a total cutie.

After Christina gave her notice, I called Desirée.

"So, Desirée, how'd you like to become Jack's full-time nanny?"

"Yes," she enthusiastically said. "When do I start?"

"Tomorrow," I said, jokingly. "But you can wait until next week."

It's said that things happen for a reason, both good and bad. With all the life-altering events in my life, I'm a true believer in that statement. If Christina hadn't decided to follow her passion, we'd never have met Desirée. And I'd be in AA after the stress of finding a new, trustworthy nanny to care for Jack.

Being Jack's full-time nanny became the right job for her at the right time. Desirée quickly became a member of our family, more like a daughter, and remains so today. While Christina was the perfect first nanny for Jack, and we appreciated how hard she worked, I never felt the connection to her like I do with Desirée. To be fair, being a first-time mom, I didn't know what to expect in having a stranger in my home caring for my newborn.

"We need backups, so Desirée won't suffer burnout and leave us," I told Adam.

"At least there are more sites to search," Adam replied.

Fortunately, in the year since we'd hired Christina and Desirée, several new nanny/babysitter sites had launched, so I had a larger pool of profiles to choose from. Desirée remained our primary nanny, but we slowly added more young women on standby to give her much-needed breaks.

"Jack has his own harem," I'd always tell Adam. "And you realize, based on their ages, each could be our daughter?"

While Jack's nannies came from different backgrounds, the one thing they all had in common was that they loved Jack and his cute personality and infectious smile.

. . .

Kelly, a friend of Desirée's, came from Toronto. She had a sweet King Charles Cavalier named Charlotte. When not caring for children, Kelly was a talented photographer and always had her camera. I marveled at her energy and enthusiasm, and I swear I never saw her without a smile on her face.

Lizzie, a former Miss North Carolina, was a beautiful young blonde woman who went on to become a successful TV meteorologist in North Carolina and Florida. Several years later, while on a family road trip, we passed through North Carolina on our way home. Lizzie was working at a television station in Raleigh-Durham, so we visited her at work, where she let Jack be on set with her. She's now a mom of three.

Renée, an actress and part-time player for Sesame Street Workshop, was a military brat from Texas. She married an actual rocket scientist and is now a mom of four.

Julianne, an undergraduate of Johns Hopkins, was applying to law school when we first met her.

"Where do you want to go to law school?" we asked.

"I've been accepted to Harvard, University of Virginia, Yale, and Penn. I'm waiting to hear from Columbia and NYU," she told us. "I'm hoping to go to NYU to stay in the city."

Adam and I just sat in awe of her and her brilliance. Fortunately, she got accepted at NYU and found time to keep babysitting for Jack, mainly while she studied for big exams. She's now a mom to an adorable son.

Sidney, an artist and an undergraduate from UCLA, received her master's from Yale. Unfortunately, her artistic talents didn't rub off on Jack. Still, our arts and crafts supply immensely expanded while she worked with us. She's now a mom of two boys.

And then there was Sarah, a professional musician with the voice of an angel. There wasn't a request Jack made that Sarah didn't fulfill. She took him around New York City like he was her own child. Jack went through his exploration phase with Sarah and became obsessed with our apartment building's elevators and stairwells.

"You know Jack and Sarah are walking up and down the stairs all day?" Esad, our building concierge, told me when I came home from work one night. "I hope she's okay with that."

"That's Sarah," I told him. "She'll do anything for Jack."

One afternoon, while I was working from home, Sarah brought Jack to her new apartment building to show him around. They ventured up to the rooftop deck. Because the building was more modern than ours, the doors taking you out to the rooftop deck had an automatic seal, keeping the air inside. As Jack played with the open and close mechanism to the door, he didn't realize his hand was in the way, and the door automatically closed on his fingers.

Back at my apartment, while on a conference call, I received a frantic call from Sarah.

"Jack slammed his hand in the door, and it's swelling, and he's so upset," Sarah said.

She was crying hysterically.

"Sarah, it's okay. Please calm down so I can understand what you're saying," I said.

"I'm going to bring him home right now," she said.

Sarah and Jack arrived home about twenty minutes later. Thinking she took a taxi from her apartment, I didn't understand why she was so sweaty and breathless when she busted through the front door.

"What happened to you?" I asked her. "You're out of breath. Sit down and have some water."

"I couldn't find a taxi, so I carried Jack the entire way," she said.

Sarah's apartment, located at West 57th Street and 11th Avenue, sat about a mile from my apartment at West 67th Street and Amsterdam Avenue. And she practically ran the entire way, carrying a screaming, forty-pound five-year-old.

I could barely inspect Jack's hand because he was screaming and crying. He wouldn't let me look, but I could see it was as swollen as a balloon. I just knew he had broken one or more fingers.

Complicating matters, Jack has mild hemophilia, a bleeding disorder where the blood doesn't clot as fast as in someone who doesn't have hemophilia. When Jack was first diagnosed, the doctor explained that we should be concerned with what we can't see rather than what we can see. In other words, surface scrapes like skinned knees and paper cuts aren't as severe for him. But smashed hands and swollen fingers are serious. I quickly called Jack's hematologist, Dr. Hurlet, to tell her what had happened.

"Take him immediately to the emergency room," she said. "I'll call ahead so you won't have to wait."

"Why is his hand so swollen?" I asked. "Do you think it's broken?"

"They'll take X-rays to confirm whether or not anything is broken," she said. "But most likely, the swelling is blood pooling around the area he got caught in the door."

Poor Jack. And poor Sarah. She was so upset, but this wasn't her fault. I remained calm throughout the entire ordeal. I don't know if my calmness had to do with being in shock about what had happened or because, being older, I understood sometimes accidents can and will occur. I fully trusted Sarah, as I did all our sitters. I also had the wisdom of many mom friends who prepared me for such moments.

"Judy, don't worry over things you can't control," many friends told me. "Don't freak out every time Jack injures himself, or you'll spend his entire childhood panicking and trying to figure out how to bubble wrap him." I now understood what they meant and was thankful to be the recipient of older mom knowledge.

"I'm coming with you to the emergency room," Sarah said. "I don't want to leave Jack."

"Are you sure?" I asked. "It's so late, and you've been through a lot today."

"No, I'm coming with you," she said.

I called Adam while he was driving home from work and explained what had happened.

"How long until you're home?" I asked him. "I need to take Jack to the ER."

"It will be faster for you to take a taxi," he said. "I'll meet you there."

Because Dr. Hurlet had called ahead, they took us to a room as soon as we arrived at the ER. As I filled out the paperwork, a hospital worker came to ask me questions.

"What happened?" she asked me. "Was this an accident?"

"Yes, it was an accident," I replied, wondering what she thought had happened. "My son got his hand caught in a door."

"I see from our records that you've brought your son here before because of an accident," she said.

She was referring to the prior year's incident when Jack was four and hit his head on our end table, giving himself a concussion. And then it dawned on me. The woman didn't think this was an accident. Fortunately, my filter was on, and I didn't say anything that would have indeed meant a visit from Child Protective Services or gotten me arrested. But there was so much I wanted to say.

"I swear this was an accident," Sarah told the hospital worker. And then Sarah went on to describe what happened in detail. She started crying again.

"It's all okay," I told her. "Don't worry about anything."

The technician finally came and took Jack to x-ray his hand.

"No, Mommy, no. I don't want to get an X-ray," Jack screamed.

"It's okay, honey," I assured him. "They're just going to take a picture of your hand."

This calmed him down and he allowed the man to take the X-ray. Of course, the technician let him play with some of the buttons on the machine, the perfect distraction for a five-year-old.

Fortunately, nothing was broken, and as Dr. Hurlet had assumed, the swelling had come from blood pooling around the area where Jack had smashed his hand in the door.

While we waited to be discharged, Sarah's phone rang. It was her mother.

"Is everything okay?" I asked Sarah when she hung up the phone.

"Yes," she said. "My mother tracks my phone, and when she didn't hear from me, she got worried because she saw I was at Mount Sinai Hospital."

"It doesn't matter how old you are, mothers always worry about their babies," I said.

She nodded and smiled for the first time since she busted through my front door with Jack.

Today, Sarah is a wonderful mom to two beautiful daughters. I'm sure she'll worry as much about them as I do about Jack, and as much as her mom worries about her.

The Michelin-Starred Child-Friendly Restaurant

PORTABILITY IS ONE OF the most remarkable things about raising an infant in New York City. You can take the baby anywhere, including busy venues, bars, and even Michelin-starred restaurants.

When Jack was a newborn and I was working full-time, I didn't have any friends with newborns. All my friends had older kids. One cold January evening, Hannah, one of my closest friends who lived in Connecticut, threw a party to celebrate her youngest daughter's seventh birthday at Mars 2110, a restaurant in Midtown Manhattan.

Adam and I decided to join the party and wish Riley a happy birthday. With Jack barely two months old, we were starved for adult conversation. When we arrived at the restaurant, we walked into a futuristic-themed establishment that felt like we were walking into a dark underground club where your feet stuck to the floor from spilled food and drinks. And it had a mildew smell. With Jack bundled up in his stroller, we made our way to the large round table filled with Hannah and her girlfriends and their children.

"Give me the baby," said Hannah.

"I want to hold him," another mom said.

And one by one, Hannah's friends held Jack and passed him around like a football.

These women were beyond the infant stage with their children, and I could tell from their desire to hold Jack that they missed this phase of motherhood. Jack seemed content, being handled and held by multiple people, but then he began to cry.

"Where's his binkie?" I asked Adam as I frantically searched his stroller. "I had three in here, and now there are none."

Hannah shined her phone's flashlight on the table to help me locate the missing binkie. She pointed it underneath the table when I didn't find it among all the wine glasses.

"Oh gross," I said. "The binkie is under the table."

One of Hannah's friends quickly grabbed the filthy binkie from my hand, dipped it into her wine glass, and swooshed it around.

"There," she said. "Now it's sterilized."

And then she put it in Jack's mouth. Everyone started laughing, and at first, I almost passed out thinking about Jack sucking on a binkie found underneath a table in a sticky, dirty public place. But then I thought about the combined parental experience of the ladies sitting around the table and how it far surpassed my less than two months. Being an older parent, you're either uptight about everything, or you go with the flow and let your experienced friends lead the way. I sat in the latter category. As a bonus, with the added flavor from the wine, Jack slept through the night, and so did Adam and I.

. . .

Blue Ribbon Sushi, the scene of my first date with Adam, became one of our favorite restaurants in the city. The sushi is phenomenal, and we became friendly with the managers and staff because we frequented the restaurant.

A few months after Jack was born, my best friend, Melinda, who lived in Houston, came to New York to help me. We took her to Blue Ribbon to thank her for all her help and to treat her to our favorite sushi restaurant. We placed Jack's infant carrier on the ground next to our table, and he quickly fell asleep, allowing us to enjoy a fantastic sushi meal. While we were eating, one of the managers stopped by our table.

"It's so great to see you both and meet your little man!" he said. "He's adorable, and I hope you'll introduce him to sushi soon."

After we finished our meal, the waiter brought our check, and Adam shook his head when he looked at the bill.

"There seems to be a mistake on my bill," he told the waiter. "There's no charge."

Right about that time, the manager came over.

"The meal is on us," he said. "You're two of our best customers, and this is our way of congratulating you on the birth of your son."

We were shocked. And a little upset we hadn't ordered more.

"This is too much," we said. "And so nice of you."

"I trust you'll keep coming back," the manager said with a wink.

And we would come back.

In fact, we went back the following weekend. This time, a different manager, who we also knew, was working.

"How wonderful to see you both and meet this precious baby," he said.

The manager didn't comp our meal that night, but he served several chef-favorite appetizers on the house.

"Should we try for the third weekend in a row?" I asked Adam.

"Let's not push our luck," he said.

. . .

On another occasion, I made a reservation at a Michelin-rated restaurant. I didn't consider whether it was a child-friendly place or if Jack would be welcome. Being older and childless when we first got together, Adam and I frequented the best restaurants in New York City and rarely went to child-friendly establishments.

"I made a reservation at Café Boulud," I told Adam.

"Will they let Jack in?" Adam asked.

"I have no idea, but why not?" I said. "He won't take up much space."

When we arrived at the restaurant, the hostess gave me a curious look when she saw me coming with a baby. She said nothing at first, but her sneer said it all: this wasn't a child-friendly restaurant. Then she finally spoke.

"I suppose you'll need a high chair?" she asked as she turned up her nose.

"Yes, that would be great," I said with a smile.

This wasn't the time for me to be snarky. As the hostess walked us to our table, I decided to ignore the glares and stares from other diners. Adam and I ordered wine, appetizers, and a main beef entrée that we split. As we enjoyed our meal, Jack, sitting in his high chair placed at the head of the booth table, feasted on his bottle and Cheerios I packed for the occasion, and smiled and charmed all the waitstaff and customers who passed by.

"Your baby is so well-behaved," one customer said on their way out of the restaurant. "I barely noticed he was here."

"Your baby has better manners than some of our customers," our waitress commented. "Please bring him back soon."

When we left the restaurant, I gave the snooty hostess a big grin as I strolled Jack away. I guess a Michelin-starred restaurant is child-friendly after all.

It's Only Pre-K

FOR PARENTS EVERYWHERE ELSE but in New York City, applying to preschool means filling out an application and writing a check to pay for it. But in New York City, the competition for getting your child into a "good" preschool is akin to applying to college. For some schools, registration begins before the ink from the footprint is dry on the child's birth certificate. When it came time to enroll Jack in pre-K, I called a few schools in my neighborhood. I didn't understand how to play the game and naively assumed I'd have my pick of schools to choose from for Jack. Wrong.

"Once you fill out our application, you wait to hear from us to schedule your parent interview," the admissions director from a neighborhood school told me. "Then you and your child will come in for an interview."

"You do realize he's three years old?" I asked the woman. I assumed she fielded at least a hundred calls like mine daily, so I cut her some slack. But this felt more like a job interview for parents than screening children for preschool, essentially daycare.

"Yes, but competition is fierce at our school," she replied. "We receive hundreds of applications for only a handful of slots."

One day, while Jack was playing in the park, I overheard some young women who looked like yoga instructors, not moms, chattering about preschool admissions. My ears perked up.

"I'm so stressed with all the applications and essays I have to fill out for preschool," said yoga mom number one, whose status-wielding Hermès Birkin doubled as the diaper bag.

"I know what you mean," said Pilates mom number two, whose monogrammed Goyard also doubled as her baby bag.

"How many schools have you applied to?" asked the Birkin mom. "We've applied to at least five."

"It's the same with us," the Goyard mom said. But I hope we get into Temple Emanu-El's nursery program because it's one of the best."

Adam and I were members of Temple Emanu-El, so hearing how coveted the school was to the Goyard mom gave me hope. Our membership would count for something in their decision process, right? Wrong, again.

After I filled out the rigorous application for Temple Emanu-El's preschool, I received a letter with an interview date. I took the day off from work to attend. On the morning of the interview, a snowstorm blanketed the city. I called the school to confirm our appointment.

"With the snowstorm today, are you still conducting preschool interviews?" I asked the receptionist.

"Oh yes!" she said. "No one would ever let a little weather prevent them from this interview. Rescheduling is often harder than scheduling."

An hour before the interview, I strolled Jack to the bus stop to wait for the bus that would take us across Central Park to Temple Emanu-El. I left Jack in the stroller as we waited, and he fell asleep.

No buses came to our stop. I frantically searched for a taxi to drive us across the park. Hailing a taxi during a rainstorm in New York City is nearly impossible, and finding a cab after a snowstorm is equally challenging. With the clock ticking, I knew my only option was to walk across Central Park in hopes of arriving as close to my scheduled time as possible. With Jack bundled up and sleeping soundly in his stroller, I speed-walked along the 66th Street Transverse through the park. This narrow outlet, designed mainly for cars to drive from the west to the east side of Manhattan, also had a skinny sidewalk for pedestrians looking for a more direct path and a safer route than the park's snow-covered winding hills and valleys.

When I arrived at Temple Emanu-El, after being splashed by speeding cars along the transverse, I looked like a wet rat with bright red cheeks, teary eyes from the wind, and a mascara-stained face. Making matters worse, Jack had just awoken from his nap and started crying.

"Would you like some water and a tissue?" the kind security guard asked me as I wheeled Jack's stroller into the lobby. "You look a little frazzled," she said.

"Yes, thank you," I said breathlessly. "It's cold out there, and buses and taxis seemed unavailable today."

After I collected myself and wiped off the mascara from my cheeks, the security guard directed me to the elevators.

"Just take the elevator to the second floor, and someone will greet you," she said. "Good luck."

She knew I needed it.

A woman with a toothy grin greeted me as I exited the elevator.

"Hello, you must be Judy. And this must be your son, Jack."

And then she looked me over from head to toe and said, "We're so happy to have you today. My goodness, you look like you walked here."

"I did," I said. I wanted to say, "I gave my driver the day off," but then decided my sarcasm probably wouldn't help Jack's chances.

Technically, the "interview" process was more of a playgroup, so two other children joined Jack, along with their very young parents and what appeared to be a nanny. All seemed unaffected by the weather outside. They hadn't given their drivers the day off.

We walked into a small classroom with buckets and bins of books, blocks, and educational toys. A woman, who I assumed was the teacher, told us to sit with our child on the rug in the center of the room. As I took my seat, Jack made a beeline toward the back of the room.

"Mommy, tiny toilets," he said. And then he proceeded to flush the tiny toilets over and over again.

During the timeframe for these interviews, Jack had started potty training and had become obsessed with all things related to toilets.

"Jack, please come sit down, and let's play with the toys," I begged him while smiling at the teacher and other adults in the room. "He's recently started potty training, so he's very curious about all this."

As the teacher reviewed her agenda, the other children sat nicely with their parents or nanny and played with age-appropriate toys. More than once, the teacher had to ask me to have Jack step away from the tiny toilets.

When we got home, I called Adam at work.

"Well, if they're looking for a child who will sit on the floor and play nicely with his toys, I'm not sure Jack made an excellent impression," I said. "But, if they're looking for a janitor, we're in!"

Based on Jack's obsession with tiny toilets, I did not think that he would be a future alum of Temple Emanu-El Nursery School. But I wasn't upset or worried. We would find another preschool. Besides, I'd rather a school accept Jack for his curiosity and thirst for knowledge than his ability to sit and obey like a trained dog.

.   .   .

One afternoon, our nanny, Desirée, took Jack to a playground near our apartment, and walking back home, she noticed a small school called Woodside Preschool, and took a brochure. Woodside is a part of the Dwight School, a private school on the Upper West Side.

Desirée told me, "You should fill out an application just to get his name in the mix."

"Okay," I said. "I wonder if the classrooms have tiny toilets."

I filled out the application and emailed it to the admissions office. A few days later, I received a call from the admissions director to schedule an interview.

Like the day of our interview at the temple, another snowstorm hit the city. I called to confirm our appointment and learned that while several families canceled their interviews, the school was still conducting appointments. Rescheduling wasn't an issue for Woodside like it was for Temple Emanu-El.

Because the school was close to our apartment, I decided to keep our appointment. We shared the room with two other children and their parents/nanny. While everyone again appeared younger than I was, I didn't feel the uptightness I felt at the temple's nursery school.

"Mommy, another tiny toilet!" Jack exclaimed upon walking into the room.

Here we go again.

"He's potty training and is a little obsessed," I explained to the director.

"That's totally fine. It's good to see he's curious," she said.

I loved her. She had zero judgment for Jack and his weirdness about plumbing.

The interview went well, and I hoped the school would accept Jack into their Threes program. Then we received a call from the admissions office.

"We loved Jack and would love to have him and your family be part of our community, but unfortunately, we don't have space right now," she said. "Would you like to go on our waiting list?"

Oh well. The teachers weren't looking for a plumbing apprentice, after all.

"Yes, we'd love to stay on your waiting list. Please let me know if or when there's movement."

I went back to the drawing board to find another option.

One afternoon, while I sat on the park benches watching Jack play on the jungle gym, I overheard a woman speaking to other mothers about a new preschool she was opening near our apartment. I asked her for a flyer.

At dinner that night, I told Adam about it. "A woman handed me a flyer today about a new preschool she's opening near Riverside Park. She used to be a teacher and is starting a more hands-on approach to education. I'll give her a call."

After speaking to the school's admissions director, I made an appointment to tour the facility and gather more information. When I arrived, I noticed it wasn't exactly a school or a traditional setting. It was in the basement of an old brownstone at the corner of West 79th Street and Riverside Drive, more precisely, across the street to the entrance to the West Side Highway, one of the busiest highway on-ramps in Manhattan.

As I walked through the rusty front gate of the building, I saw a man entering.

"Are you here for the preschool tour?" he asked.

"Yes. Am I in the right place?"

He said I was, so I followed him down a dark, dank hallway with a distinctive smell of mildew. It felt more like a dungeon than a preschool.

"Hi, welcome to our new preschool," a cheery woman said as she greeted me. "I trust you found us okay?"

"Yes, but I needed help getting in once I got here. But this nice young man assisted me."

"David is one of our teachers. He helps me with the curriculum," she said.

Looking around the small space, I noticed three kids sitting at a table coloring a piece of paper.

"Are these your students?" I asked.

"Yes. We're still in our ramp-up phase."

I secretly wondered if the children were related to the director. I realized there was a start-up phase for every business and school. Still, the price tag associated with this new school rivaled one semester at an Ivy League university. For the money, I would have hoped a bright, cheery space filled with the latest educational toys would surround the children as they learned how to hold a fork and tie their shoes. Instead, this room reminded me of a spooky Grimms' Fairy Tale scene.

I thanked the director for her time and told her I'd be in touch.

I updated Adam on the tour over dinner that night.

"Maybe we need to leave the city. Or we need to find a daycare where I can drop off Jack in the morning and pick him up after work."

"It's only pre-K. We'll find something," he said.

A few days later, I visited a daycare facility close to our apartment. Although it called itself a pre-K school, it had all the markings of a drop-off center. I took a tour and went home to tell Adam about my thoughts.

"Jack will be happy at this place because there are toys everywhere, a playground across the street, and several tiny toilets to flush."

We decided to enroll Jack in this daycare facility, but right before I emailed my application, the admissions director at Woodside Preschool called me.

"We have an opening in the afternoon Threes program if you're still interested."

"Yes, we are very interested!" I replied.

And like that, Jack's schooling adventure began. Fortunately, I didn't have to go through the exhaustive application process to get Jack into another school after pre-K. The Dwight School is a pre-K–12 institution, so all I had to do was tell them we were continuing and write another check.

Even with my excitement for Jack's new adventure, the irony of my friends' Facebook posts of their children starting high school and college while I shared photos of Jack entering pre-K was not lost on me. When the time came for me to post high school photos of Jack, most of my friends would be grandparents or soon-to-be grandparents.

And then there was the age difference between the moms of kids in Jack's class and me. The good news was that even though the spread was anywhere from eight to fourteen years, I showed great pride in taking exceptional care of myself, especially my skin. No one believed I was as old as I was. The only exception was the young mother who had her daughter at age twenty, and her mother had her at age twenty as well. That meant I was older than the grandmother. I only prayed people wouldn't ask me if Jack was my grandson.

The Lonely Phone Booth

WHEN JACK WAS ABOUT four, he informed me he had a wife. I'd always heard children developed wild imaginations and sometimes had imaginary friends. I just never thought one of Jack's first would become my daughter-in-law.

"Who is she, and where does she live?" I asked, thinking it was the cute little blonde from his preschool class.

"Her name is Ugg," he said. "She's a hundred and three and lives in Florida."

"Where did you meet her?" I asked, curious.

"In New York City," he said.

"Were you at the park when you met her?" I continued.

"Yes. Ugg's apartment is on West End Avenue and West 100th Street, near the park," he said.

"But I thought you said she lived in Florida?" I asked, trying to get more information.

"She's a snowbird, like Grammy's friends," he said.

My mother lived in Florida full-time, but many of her friends lived there part-time, making them "snowbirds."

"How do you know Ugg lives on West End Avenue and West 100th Street? Have you been to her apartment?" I asked, praying the answer was no.

"Because that's where she lives, Mommy," he matter-of-factly said, again proving he got his smart mouth from me.

I had recently purchased a new pair of Ugg snow boots and had taken Jack to the store with me. This shopping excursion led me to believe this is when the idea of Ugg was born.

. . .

One of my favorite things about living and raising a child in New York City is identifying places featured in movies, television programs, books, and songs. I've always been a creature of pop culture. There's nothing better than listening to Billy Joel's "New York State of Mind" and knowing every place he mentions in the song. And I love that I can be walking around places like Riverside Park and stand in the very spot where Meg Ryan's and Tom Hanks' characters finally realized they were in love in *You've Got Mail*. Or just a few blocks down, I recognize the place where they found a dead body floating in the Hudson River on a *Law & Order SVU* episode. It's all so incredible.

So, imagine my surprise when I opened one of those daily deal emails that lure you into buying something you don't need and saw an offer for a children's book about a phone booth in New York City at the corner of West End Avenue and West 100th Street.

Author Peter Ackerman wrote *The Lonely Phone Booth*. The idea for the children's book came to him when his then three-year-old son, walking near West End Avenue and West 100th Street, asked about the box on the corner. That simple question inspired Ackerman to write a wonderful children's book told from the perspective of the phone booth, and the Manhattan Children's Theatre even turned the story into a play.

"Jack, you'll never believe the new book I found today about a phone booth located at the corner of West End Avenue and West 100th Street," I said. "It's called *The Lonely Phone Booth*. Have you read it?"

Based on Jack's precise location of Ugg's apartment, I believed he'd previously read this book in school or at a friend's house, but when I showed him the email, he claimed he'd never seen it.

"But honey, if you haven't read the book, how did you know this was the corner where Ugg's apartment is located?" I asked.

"Because I told you, Mommy, that's where she lives," he said.

"Did you make it up?" I asked.

"Yes," he said.

I quit trying to rationalize where Jack came up with this location.

Then he asked, "Mommy, what's a phone booth, and can we go see it?"

In true New York City fashion, Adam, Jack, and I went on an adventure to the corner of West End Avenue and West 100th Street, and sure enough, there it stood: "the lonely phone booth." The building was under scaffolding, also in true New York City fashion.

I couldn't believe it, and neither could Adam.

"What are the chances?" Adam asked.

"I know!" I said. "Jack and I don't hang out up here; the street is thirty-three blocks north of our apartment."

"Look, Mommy, there it is," Jack said. "How does it work?"

"Well," I said, "before cell phones, if you needed to call someone and weren't in your house or at work, you could slip into a phone booth, put a dime in the slot, and make a call."

He stared at me in amazement.

"I'm not sure this phone works anymore," I said. "Plus, it's filthy in there, so don't touch anything."

My last warning came too late. Jack immediately jumped into the booth, picked up the phone, and tried calling—you guessed it: Ugg. She wasn't home.

We walked to the subway after Jack posed for pictures inside the phone booth. And we talked about the relics the whole way home. At the time, Manhattan's last four remaining phone booths were located on the Upper West Side: West End Avenue and West 66th Street, West End Avenue and West 90th Street, West End Avenue and West 101st Street, and the "lonely phone booth" at West End Avenue and West 100th Street.

"The phone booth is cool," he said. "But why would anyone use one when an iPhone is so much easier?"

"Precisely why Steve Jobs became a billionaire," I said.

I gave up on understanding why or how Jack created the address for Ugg's apartment and the coincidence of its precise location with the phonebooth from the book. I did wonder, however, if this meant Jack had a future as a television and movie location scout in New York City.

A few months later, I asked Jack how Ugg was doing.

"We're no longer married," he said.

"Why, what happened?" I asked.

"She died," he said. "She got too old."

"I'm sorry," I said. "Have you met anyone else?"

"No, I'm too young," he said. "But I've got time."

"Yes, you do," I said. "Yes, you do."

I wondered where Jack's next wife would live. Given his imagination, I hoped he'd pick a more exciting place to visit like Hawaii or Europe, rather than a street corner on the Upper West Side of Manhattan, next to a dirty old phone booth.

The Polar Vortex

GROWING UP IN TEXAS, I'd heard a common saying: "If you don't like the weather, just wait thirty minutes and it will change." Of course, this usually refers to sunshine and rain, not snow.

When I was nine, it snowed in Houston. This historical event closed schools and businesses. At the time, I'd only seen snow when visiting relatives in New Jersey, so this was a big deal.

"Judy, wake up," my mother said. "It's snowing outside, and school is canceled."

The three best words told to a child are "school is canceled."

Celia and I bundled up in our winter coats, hats, and mittens and then ran outside. While the snow barely covered the ground, we still managed to gather enough to make snowballs and pelt each other in the face.

"Let's make snow ice cream," my mother announced. "Help me scoop up enough to put in the freezer before it melts."

Later that afternoon, after we had spent all day outside playing in the barely one-inch snow on the ground, my mother called us inside.

"Would you like chocolate syrup on your ice cream?" she asked.

Was that a real question? Celia and I were so happy eating our snow ice cream. And then my mother saw the afternoon newspaper headline: "Don't Eat the Snow Due to Harmful Pollutants."

Oh well. It couldn't be any worse than eating mud pie.

. . .

Snowstorms in New York City are only historical events if the media hypes them to sound worse than they are.

In 2012, New York City experienced several polar vortex winter storms. According to meteorologists on television, a polar vortex is a unique series of events in which frigid air from the north clashes with warmer air from the south. Then, the Earth, planets, sun, and stars unite. Truth: it's just plain cold outside. With a massive snowstorm forecast for the next day, I thought about the Texas winter storm of 1973 and asked Adam, "Do you think they'll close the schools?"

"I doubt it," he said. "They'll start clearing the streets once the snow stops falling."

Later that evening, we received a call from the school. The verdict: school was canceled.

But Jack and I wouldn't get to enjoy a fun snow day. As the snow began to fall outside and the temperature dropped, so did Jack's little blue eyes and energy level.

"Are you okay?" I asked him as I put him to bed.

"I don't feel good," he said.

"Is it your stomach?"

"No, I'm hot."

I felt his forehead, and it was on fire. I got the thermometer and took his temperature.

"It's 102.9," I told Adam. "I guess it's a good thing school is closed."

Twenty-four hours later, the snow had stopped, and the kids were back in school. But Jack still had a fever, so I called the doctor.

"Jack isn't feeling well and has had a fever for more than twenty-four hours," I told the receptionist. "I'm calling to see if the doctor can send a prescription to the pharmacy."

"No, the doctor would like to see Jack in person," she replied.

Oh great. Do you know what it's like taking your child to the doctor when it's ten degrees outside and his temperature is hovering near one hundred and three?

To add insult to injury, we couldn't find a taxi, and the ground felt as slick as an ice-skating rink. I knew we'd both hit the pavement if I rolled his stroller over one of the many patches of black ice on the sidewalks. I missed my car in these moments.

After I pushed Jack's stroller through whipping winds, dodging pedestrians on the sidewalks, and avoiding the ice, we finally arrived at the doctor's office. I stripped Jack of his layers and discarded my own as we waited to be called back.

After examining him, the doctor said, "It appears Jack has your typical kids' virus that needs to run its course."

"Is there anything I can give him or do to help keep him calm when he gets restless?" I asked.

"You can drink a couple of glasses of wine, and then you won't care!" she said.

I loved Jack's doctor. She got me.

Later that evening, after I put Jack to bed, I had a big glass of wine.

"Doctor's orders," I told Adam.

Even though Jack suffered from "typical" kid viruses, he was barely sick as a child. As a former boss once told me, "Sometimes it's better to be lucky than good." I often thought this when I saw so many of my friends' children experience viruses, pink eye, strep throat, norovirus, and other illnesses that would take down the entire household.

Of course, maybe exposing Jack to dirt had something to do with our "luck." I'd often question why people asked you to remove your shoes upon entering their homes.

"Should we take off our shoes?" asked everyone who came to our apartment.

"Why?" I'd always respond.

"To keep out all the filth from the dirty New York City streets," they'd say.

This practice reminded me of a *Sex and the City* episode when Carrie was asked to remove her Jimmy Choo shoes before entering a friend's apartment, and her shoes were stolen by another guest. It never dawned on me to ask someone to remove their shoes before entering my home. I get the logic, but how else do you expose your kids to germs and build their immune systems? This doesn't mean I keep a dirty home; quite the contrary. But I don't freak out if some dirt and grime make their way inside. No judgment, but isn't this why Swiffer mops were invented?

In my youth, I never took my shoes off in the house. I made (and sometimes ate) dirt pies. I feasted on PB&J sandwiches. I blame a lot of the world's problems today on our nut-free society. That's not to say peanut allergies don't exist and aren't potentially deadly for people who are allergic, but for those who aren't allergic, let them eat peanuts!

When Jack was about two, I took him to a Central Park playground. I sat talking to other moms and nannies as our children climbed jungle gyms and ran around like cheetahs. I looked over at Jack sitting in the sandbox. I thought, essentially prayed, *Jack, don't you do it!* As the words went through my head, Jack, with a Cheshire cat grin, scooped up two handfuls of sand and shoved them into his mouth. I thought I'd pass out.

I grabbed him from the sandbox and rammed my hands in his mouth, frantically getting out as much sand as possible. I kept thinking about all the things lurking inside the sand that were now inside my son's system. I almost took him straight to the pediatrician for a tetanus shot. But then, I thought that if this didn't boost his immune system, what would?

Now, I'm not an advocate for eating sand in Central Park as a preventive method. But as an observation, Jack had fewer colds and viruses than his friends. Coincidence? Luck? I'll never know.

We Live on an Island

I REMEMBER READING and watching YouTube videos about infant survival swimming, the practice of throwing a baby in a swimming pool and hoping it would naturally float to its back. It sounded horrible and freaked me out. But after Jack began swimming lessons, the concept intrigued me. By choosing this method, a parent never goes through the unbearable pain of dragging their kid to swim lessons only to have them scream the whole way there and continue screaming throughout the class as they cling on for dear life to the swim teacher's neck.

Growing up in Houston, Texas, I didn't have a swimming pool in my backyard. Instead, my parents had a pool membership at the Royal Coach Inn, a roadside hotel off the Southwest Freeway. This fine establishment was also called the "Roach Coach Inn" or the "Royal Roach Inn." I don't need to elaborate past those names. Kids were offered swim lessons during the summertime, and my parents took full advantage.

One weekend, my cousin, Fred, joined my parents, sister, and me for an afternoon by the pool. I couldn't wait to show off what I'd learned and demonstrate my superior swimming skills.

Before my mother could slather sunscreen over my body and firmly attach my floating device, I jumped into the water. It wasn't until I landed in the middle of the pool that I realized I didn't know as much as I thought. I started to sink lower, gasping for air. My dad and Fred sprang into action.

"Judy, hang on!" they screamed as they jumped into the water to save me.

I clearly needed more lessons.

. . .

We started introducing Jack to the swimming pool at about five months old. He liked it and didn't even cry.

He's a natural!

Living in an older New York City apartment building with scarce amenities, we didn't have the luxury of a swimming pool. Hence, Jack's encounters with a pool were relegated to summer vacations and trips to Florida to stay with Grammy and Papa. My first attempt at teaching Jack to swim was when he had just turned four. A mom from Jack's pre-K class and I decided to put the boys in a semi-private lesson at a health club in a nearby apartment building. That was a big, huge, ginormous mistake!

The pool deck was overrun with kids of all ages taking lessons simultaneously. Each class lasted only thirty minutes, and all lessons started and ended together. In other words, it was complete chaos. A few minutes before the end of the thirty-minute lessons, a man screamed into a bullhorn: "Two minutes, two minutes!" This would ensure all the kids and parents knew the class was almost over. In reality, it meant all the kids stormed the locker room at the same time.

Making matters worse, neither Jack nor his friend was confident in the water. Neither one wanted to get in the water or let go of the instructor. At one point, to pry Jack's death grip from around her neck, the instructor tossed him into the middle of the pool. As I watched

Jack fly through the air and land in the water, I thought that was it: *Great, now I'll never get him back in the pool.*

I dreaded taking Jack to his weekly swim lessons. On more than one occasion, I made his babysitter, Julianne, take him. Julianne began babysitting Jack when she moved back to New York City from Los Angeles. When we first met her, she had started applying to law schools and had plenty of time to devote to babysitting. Because of her calm disposition and love for Jack, I knew she'd be able to encourage him to go to his lesson and also persuade him to get in the water.

"I can't bear taking Jack to swim lessons today," I told her. "Will you please take him?"

"No problem," she said. "I've got this."

When they returned home, she looked frazzled.

"You weren't kidding," she said. "I don't know how Jack, or anyone, will ever learn to swim in that zoo. It's total pandemonium."

"I told you," I said. "Why do you think I sent you?"

After that experience, I put swimming on hold for several months. I revisited swim lessons in April before Jack started at the Dwight School's summer day camp program at the end of June. The camp ran for six weeks, and daily swim lessons were part of the program. I had to prepare Jack or risk him never going in the water. I heard about a fantastic swim teacher named Kim (Swim Kim) from a mom in my apartment building. I spoke to Swim Kim on the phone ahead of the first lesson.

"Jack struggled when he first took swim lessons," I explained to Kim. "And now I'm afraid he won't return to the water."

She stopped me and said, "Judy, I will have him swimming in ten lessons … I'm that good."

I was sold.

True to form, the first several lessons with Kim were a nightmare. Between the kicking and whining all the way to the pool, to the negotiating with Swim Kim during the entire lesson about what he'd do and not do (I swear he'll be a lawyer), I didn't think there was any chance Jack would even get in the water much less be swimming in ten lessons.

Then it happened. Suddenly Jack was in the water without crying. He listened to Kim's words. And he was swimming! And all in less than ten lessons. Yes, Swim Kim was that good.

It had been many years since I'd learned to swim or do any of the activities Jack was learning to do. I'd forgotten what those experiences and accomplishments felt like. I'd put too much pressure on Jack to learn to swim or ride a bike and on myself to ensure he mastered all the great childhood rites of passage. I hadn't wanted him to miss out. As parents, we like our kids to succeed at everything they try.

My anxiety about whether Jack would learn to swim made me feel like I had something to prove to the other moms at the pool deck. My age may have had something to do with my insecurities. But I needed to let Jack progress at his own pace while giving the right amount of encouragement. And I needed to cut myself some slack. As I told Jack at the beginning of swim lessons, "You don't need to learn how to swim like an Olympic athlete; you just need to learn how to swim. After all, we live on an island."

Like Mother, Like Son

WOODSIDE PRESCHOOL, JACK'S new school, named their classrooms after colors and animals: Gray Dolphins, Copper Sea Otters, Green Sea Turtles, and Orange Clownfish. Jack was about to become a proud Orange Clownfish. He wanted to be in that class because orange was one of his favorite colors, and honestly, on most days, he acted like a clown—a perfect match. Naturally, we bought him an orange hoodie and a stuffed orange clownfish to mark the occasion.

The morning of Jack's first day of school, he was so excited to start the day he would have run to school if I allowed him to. He, of course, wore his orange hoodie in celebration. I wondered when the excitement of going to school would stop. The first homework assignment? The first test? The first breakup?

As expected, the school was all smiles as we entered. The teachers enthusiastically welcomed everyone. Parents were allowed to take their kids into their classrooms and spend some time getting them settled. Because it was the first day, we stuck around to talk to each other and ensure our children were okay. I was there for about ten minutes when Jack approached me and said, "Say goodbye, Mommy, I want to play!"

What? Are you kidding me? Was he kicking me out of his classroom?

Right about then, his teacher approached me and said, "I'm not sure how to say this, but Jack wants you to leave so he can go play now."

I stood there, dumbfounded.

"Be happy about that. So many children have separation anxiety, but Jack doesn't appear to be one of those kids. Good job, mom!"

This reminded me of when my father took me to school on the first day of first grade. He asked if I wanted him to go inside with me, and I told him I was okay alone. I didn't know that this statement shook him to his core. I now understand why.

It's safe to say I was the one who had the separation issues that day. How's that for irony?

.   .   .

It's been fascinating to watch Jack's personality develop over the years. With Adam's looks and my mouth, he's a combination of us both. Fortunately, he also has some of our other key characteristics. From Adam: seriousness, perfectionism, kindness, and a sweet disposition. From me: silliness, determination, loyalty, and sarcasm.

Like Jack, I, too, have a mix of my parents' qualities. I inherited my friendly, always-wanting-to-help and good-natured personality from my mother. My stubbornness, easy-to-forgive/hard-to-forget but wouldn't-hurt-a-fly personality is from my father. I only wished I'd gotten some of his six-foot-four height.

However, one characteristic I'm passing on to Jack is that I have no filter. I can't help it. I'm too honest and speak the truth a little too freely. An example is when I managed Vollmer PR's New York office. The human resource department issued a 360 Review for the executive team. This process allowed the employees to share their assessment of the good and the bad about their managers.

"We love working with Judy because she speaks her mind, and you always know where you stand," said our HR director when reading the results to me.

"But on the flip side, we sometimes feel Judy is a little harsh and speaks her mind too freely."

At least I was a well-rounded manager.

I first recognized Jack's "no filter" personality trait at an end-of-school party for his pre-K class. The teachers planned a fabulous send-off in the form of an ice cream sundae party. If the kids weren't already hyped up enough knowing summer was around the corner, give them lots of sugar and send them on their way. Brilliant.

After all the singing, dancing, and sugar injections, the teachers presented each parent with a comprehensive portfolio of their child's schoolwork from the past year. The binder was filled with artwork, photos, and individual projects.

I proudly flipped through the pages as I saw the great things Jack had done throughout the year. It was terrific to see the improvement from the beginning to the end of the school year. And then I came to the page that proved to me once and for all that while Jack may look like his father, he has his mother's mouth—and lack of filter—through and through.

In the portfolio section titled "Express Yourself," the photos and projects highlighted the different activities designed to help the children learn how to express themselves to others.

Some of the projects included "mood" stamps to demonstrate how each child was feeling that day, photos of the kids writing letters to their pen pals, and pictures of them showing one piece they selected from their portfolio to share with the class. They were instructed to answer the question: "Why did you choose this piece to share with your friends?"

The answers to this specific question had varied and appropriate responses such as: "I liked it because it's sparkly," "I picked this because it's pretty," "I picked it because I love race cars," etc.

And then there was Jack's response: "Because I did." There you have it—three little words that said it all. I knew it was wrong, but I beamed with pride.

My mother told me right before Jack was born that I would have a child like me. She was correct. Jack's three little smart-aleck words reminded me of when I belonged to B'nai B'rith Youth Organization, a Jewish youth group in high school. One of the chapters hosted a beauty pageant fundraiser. My chapter nominated me to participate, even though I greatly resisted. In addition to a talent section, where most girls performed dance routines (I played the piano), there was a question-and-answer segment. The question: "If you could wish for three things, what would they be?" This was a real life-changing question for sure.

While most girls gave vague responses like "World peace" and "No wars," my answer was a little more specific: "Better grades in school, less homework, and I wish this stupid thing was over." While I got the laugh, I didn't win the pageant. My poor mother and sister wanted to run out of the auditorium and hide.

Reading Jack's sarcastic response to that simple question made me think that while I may be a lost cause and too old to learn to temper my filter, hopefully it's not too late for Jack.

Why I Color My Hair

ONE OF THE MOST significant achievements in a child's life is conquering the fear of something they believe they're too scared to do. These milestones include but are not limited to: walking, potty training, going to school, and riding a scooter or bicycle.

For parents, one of the most significant achievements is conquering the fear of *accepting* their child is doing something not only the child thought they'd be too scared to do but that we as parents are scared to have them do. These milestones include, but are not limited to: walking, potty training, going to school, and riding a scooter or bike.

Once the achievements are conquered, deciding who is more excited, or still fearful, is probably impossible. When Jack was in pre-K, scooters became so popular his school had "scooter" parking next to the strollers. Scooter riding in New York City is a big deal, and just as many adults are in on the action as kids, although they look ridiculous. A few months before Jack started riding his bicycle sans training wheels, he begged us for a scooter.

"Mommy, I want a scooter like my friends. I'm the only one who doesn't have one," Jack pleaded.

This declaration is never a good reason for a parent to give in and say yes. It reminded me of my father who would say, "If all your friends jump off the Brooklyn Bridge, does that mean you will jump too?" Of course, being a sarcastic kid, I'd typically respond with "We don't live in Brooklyn, so why would my friends jump off the bridge?" Fortunately, my father was a colossal teaser and as sarcastic as I was, so I usually got away with my smart mouth.

But back to my conversation with Jack and why I didn't want him to ride a scooter.

"I don't know, honey. They look dangerous?" I said to him.

Honestly, my fear of the scooter was more about being afraid Jack inherited my klutz gene. I worried he'd spend more time falling off than riding on it. And you'd understand my fear if you ever saw me on rollerblades or a skateboard (I don't even think they had scooters back in the olden days).

The sidewalks of New York City are on a whole different stratosphere than the flat neighborhood streets of Houston. Operating a scooter is like driving a car on the streets of Manhattan: you must be super defensive and assume pedestrians will dart before you and expect you to stop.

Watching little kids swerve in and around sidewalk traffic is a nerve-racking experience because they haven't yet learned that pedestrians have the right-of-way and they need to go around them. Of course, many adults in New York City have yet to understand that concept too.

But Adam and I finally succumbed to peer pressure and bought Jack a scooter. It was lime green, like his ASICS tennis shoes.

Our apartment building sat on West 67th Street between Broadway and Amsterdam Avenue. In front of the building, a private driveway and full courtyard connected West 67th Street to West 68th Street. The courtyard was a gathering place for residents to hang out and children to play. And it also became the ultimate obstacle course for scooter riding.

"Mommy, look at me!" he screamed, speeding down the courtyard ramp while performing one-legged tricks.

There's not enough hair color in the world to hide my fear.

Jack mastered the scooter and rode quickly, except for one big wipeout when he hit a giant crater on the sidewalk because he was going too fast.

Watching Jack's excitement about conquering his fears brought me much joy. While I marveled at his ability, knowing what a klutz I was/am, I took pride knowing he learned something independently. Of course, I'd be lying to myself if I didn't admit my heart ached at the thought of him growing up and no longer needing me. When had that happened? Had I missed it?

. . .

The summer before Jack turned five, we bought him a lime green bicycle with training wheels to match his lime green scooter and shoes. I envisioned him learning to ride quickly, like he did the scooter, and enjoying this milestone. But when Adam and I set out to teach Jack to ride his bike, we didn't calculate how long it would take him to lose the fear of being on two wheels. Yes, he'd mastered the scooter, but it sat lower to the ground.

"Mommy, I don't want to fall. I don't want boo-boos," Jack said.

"If you fall, you get back up," I told him. "And I'll kiss the boo-boos all better."

Learning to ride a bicycle includes many bumps, scrapes, and bruises. These ailments come with the territory. But the fear of getting hurt sometimes dictates the progress. And learning to ride a bike in New York City was unlike anything Adam and I had ever experienced. Growing up in Texas, one typically had big driveways, neighborhood streets, and school parking lots to perfect their riding skills, and kids rode their bikes everywhere. The sight of bikes spread all over the driveway usually meant there was trouble inside the house.

While I was never a big bike rider, I did enjoy my pink banana-seat bicycle. It was awesome, especially with the streamers on the handlebars. I remember the day the training wheels came off. With my big sister, Celia, holding on to the back of the bike, I rode down the driveway and fell on my ass within minutes. I still have that excellent coordination today.

Bike riding for Adam in Southern California was also different; he went everywhere on his bike. He never had training wheels, as his father told him to just get out and ride. And ride, he did. When we visited the neighborhood where he grew up in Los Angeles, Adam showed us around. He pointed out the streets where he'd learned to ride, and the route he'd taken to school.

New York City neighborhoods provided a different bike-riding experience than California and Texas. For starters, where would we teach Jack to ride his bike? Park Avenue, Broadway, Times Square?

One Saturday afternoon in July, Adam and I took Jack to a free bike-riding lesson for kids. The instructors took off the training wheels and pedals and guaranteed he'd be riding on two wheels by the end of the class. Several kids conquered their fears that day and rode off on two wheels. Not Jack.

We spent many weekends that same year in a parking lot in front of the famous Tavern on the Green restaurant in Central Park, trying to get Jack comfortable enough to ride.

"You can do it. You just need to ride," I said to encourage him.

"I can't, Mommy. I don't want to ride a bike."

That declaration was more about being afraid than not wanting to ride.

Finally, after several months of "practicing" in the parking lot, Jack got on his bike and rode. The training wheels came off, and he got out of his head. The next thing we knew, he was riding (and I was freaking out).

Once he was off and riding, he said, "Mommy, something just popped into my brain, and I was ready to ride!"

I'm not sure who was prouder, him or me. The more he rode, the more confidence he gained. Here's the irony: as he gained confidence, my fear increased. Is he going too fast? Will he know to get out of people's way? Will he be aware of his surroundings? And the big one: Will he get back up if he falls? For this last question, I can tell you that he did. Of course, that didn't stop me from running to his rescue. I was ready with bandages and Neosporin each time Jack fell (which he did several more times).

I'd hug him and say, "Get back up and keep going."

And he'd quickly jump back on the bike. "I'm good, Mommy."

"I know you are, honey," I'd say with a smile.

In these moments, it dawned on me what the symbolism of Jack learning to ride a bike or a scooter represented. As he grows up, he'll fall and get up many more times, but he'll learn to shake it off, get back up, and keep going. And if needed, I'll always be ready with a big hug and first aid supplies.

Superman of the Subway

WHEN PEOPLE RAISE KIDS in the suburbs, the car becomes their most essential possession. Whether driving their children to school, sports, doctor appointments, or a friend's house, they become one with their vehicle. But bringing up a child in New York City is different. If you own a car, chances are it remains in the parking garage most days. Your primary mode of transportation is your feet and the subway or bus system.

At a very young age, Jack became fascinated with trains and transportation. I printed all the subway maps, and he sat in bed most nights memorizing the lines and routes. His supreme knowledge of the MTA often impressed strangers. Jack was curious about his surroundings underground and constantly commented on one thing or another.

One afternoon, when he was barely four, we struggled to find space on the subway. Because it was the weekend, the subway car was packed. I held onto his stroller and squeezed myself between two people on the bench.

"God forbid someone give up their seat for a lady with a kid in a stroller," I later said to Adam.

As the train sped through the stations, Jack curiously looked around at all the people. Sitting across from us was a man in his twenties. He looked like he hadn't bathed or washed his hair in days.

But aside from his outward appearance, his T-shirt drew more attention.

In typical New York fashion, no one noticed him or his T-shirt except Jack.

"Mommy, why does that man's shirt say 'Mr. Right and Mr. All Night' with an arrow pointing down?" he asked me in his loudest outside voice.

The man's face turned beet red, and everyone in earshot of Jack could barely contain their laughter.

I looked at the man wearing the obnoxious T-shirt and said, "Yep, he reads."

The man exited the train as soon as it pulled into the next station. I secretly wondered if it was even his stop.

One afternoon, while shopping for clothes at Bloomingdale's, Jack incessantly talked about the subway line we took to get to the store. One of the sales associates overheard our conversation.

"Excuse me, young man. If I need to get home to Astoria, Queens, from Bloomingdale's, which subway line should I take?" he asked Jack.

I could tell he thought he'd stump this little kid.

Without missing a beat, Jack proudly told the man, "To get to Astoria, Queens, from here you would need to take the N, Q, or R train, but you can't take the Q train on weekends because the last stop is West 57th Street going uptown, and the Bloomingdale's stop is 59th Street."

Dumbfounded, the man turned to me.

"Do you live in Queens?" he asked.

"No, we live on the Upper West Side. My son is obsessed with trains and subways and has memorized all the lines and routes."

The man shook his head, but I didn't give it a second thought.

. . .

Jack and I frequently took subway adventures throughout Manhattan and the other four boroughs. We never had a particular destination in mind and decided on our routes once we got on the train. One hot summer afternoon, after we'd taken ten different trains going nowhere, I was exhausted, sweaty, and desperate to get above ground. I wanted to go home to air conditioning and a shower.

"Mommy, I want to wait for a new C train," Jack said as an older C subway car pulled into the station.

"What difference does it make if we take a newer train or an older one?" I asked him. "Let's just get home."

"No, please, let's wait for a newer train. It makes announcements at each stop, and it's cleaner," he pleaded.

I couldn't argue with the cleanliness factor of the newer train.

"Okay, but if the next train is older, we're getting on it," I said.

"Okay, fine," he reluctantly agreed.

Of course, the next train wasn't a newer version. It screeched into the station, and the doors barely opened. I wondered just how old it was. I looked down at Jack's little face as it hung in defeat.

"Okay, we'll wait for one more train, but that's it," I told him.

"Yay!" he said.

Even though my clothes stuck to my body, and I smelled like the inside of a stale subway car, how could I disappoint Jack when all he wanted to do was ride in a newer car? As we stood on the platform, deeply discussing the features of a newer train versus an older car, an MTA worker overheard our conversation.

"Excuse me, young man, I wanted to let you know the next train will be a new one, so be sure to get on it," he told Jack, then winked at me.

"Oh, thank god," I said to the man. "We've been in the subway for hours, and I'm ready to go home."

As promised, a brand-new C train arrived with the announcement: "Stand clear of the closing doors, please." Jack beamed with pride.

In addition to riding the rails, Jack liked to wear subway attire. Inside Grand Central Terminal is a small transit museum selling T-shirts, hats, stuffed animals, and other tourist-trap items displaying subway numbers and letters. Over the years, Jack collected trains for every subway line. He also proudly wore T-shirts from his favorite subways. When Jack turned seven, we bought him a number seven subway T-shirt and a stuffed bear. And you guessed it, our next subway adventure took us from Manhattan to Queens on the number seven train.

"I prefer the bus," I told Jack. "Walking up and down these stairs all day is quite the workout."

Even though I preferred taking the bus to avoid walking up and down subway stairs, I'd do anything to make Jack happy, as a mother does. The bonus to our adventures was I got to skip the leg workouts at the gym.

．　．　．

But sometimes, our subway adventures took on a life of their own. When Jack was in first grade, on one seemingly ordinary journey home from school, his friend, Lisa, and her family joined us at the West 86th Street station. We all waited on the platform with dozens of other schoolchildren and their parents and caregivers.

The B and C train lines operated out of this station, and when Jack and Lisa saw a B train pull in, they got so excited. For whatever reason, he and Lisa loved the B train. Probably because the C trains were so old and rundown that when they came into the station, the brakes screeched so loudly you wondered if the train would stop at all, much less make it to the next station.

Our normal exit for the train was the West 72nd Street station, close to where we lived. Jack pleaded with me to get off one stop past ours, at the Columbus Avenue station. This was Lisa's stop, and he liked riding with her. Who was I to come between friends?

As the train rolled into the Columbus Avenue station, we gathered all our stuff and began to exit the car. Even as seasoned as Jack was when riding the subway, we always told him to be mindful of the gap. We taught him early on to stay away from the platform edge when waiting for, entering, and exiting the train.

Unfortunately for Jack, he suffered from an inherited condition from my side of the family called "excessive talking." So, on this day, as he exited the subway, he was chatting up a storm with Lisa and wasn't mindful of the gap. And his foot and leg got stuck.

As he screamed out the words, "Mommy, my foot is stuck," not only did I have an out-of-body experience and go into superhero mode to pull him to safety, but the entire platform of people also came running to his rescue. As I grabbed him and pried his little foot free, his shoe fell off and hit the tracks.

"Oh no," he cried. "Those are my brand-new shoes."

"Honey, I don't care about your shoes. I only care about you and your safety."

As I tried to calm him down, I noticed out of the corner of my eye a man jumping up from the tracks with Jack's shoe in his hands. Now, I'll admit that once I knew Jack was safe, for a nanosecond I did think, *Damn, his new shoes.* But that was a passing thought because I couldn't have cared less about the shoe. And while I was grateful for this man's random act of kindness, I was horrified at the thought of what could have happened.

"Thank you so much," I sincerely told him. "But you really didn't need to have done that. It's so dangerous, and you could have gotten seriously hurt."

I couldn't fathom the thought of an incoming subway not seeing this man on the tracks, or worse, him being electrocuted by the third rail.

He looked at me and said, "I'm a father, and the same thing happened to my son."

The whole experience was mind numbing, and I couldn't stop thinking about the what-ifs. But since everything turned out okay, my thoughts went to the Superman of the Subway who saved my son's shoe. I prayed he'd retire his cape and never jump onto the train tracks again.

Fortunately, the MTA has retired many older trains and replaced them with high-tech computerized cars. I don't think Jack will ever lose his curiosity about the subway system, and that's okay with me. It means he'll hold onto a small part of his childhood innocence, and I'll hold onto my baby a little longer.

The Reinvention of Judy

Time for Me to Fly

MY LIFE DIDN'T FOLLOW the classic path of finding love, getting married, having a family, and building a career. Whether surviving my childhood trauma of rape, dealing with multiple family illnesses, or coping with the loss of my sister, I lived clearing one hurdle after another. It's hard to settle when life feels so unsettling. So, I ran and jumped over my twenties and thirties, the conventional age many women decide to paint the "big picture."

I've always preferred to do things in the nontraditional sense. The only thing I did early in life was talk. Therefore, it was no surprise that marriage and children became part of my plan when my friends of the same age (and younger) were celebrating ten-plus years of marriage and helping their kids study for AP and SAT exams.

I often looked on in awe at how my friends juggled mommy duties, household obligations, work commitments, and the occasional task or treat for themselves. However, that almost always seemed to be the last thing on their lists. Truth: while I was often envious that they had happy marriages, children, and fulfilling careers, I was rarely jealous of their hectic schedules and seemingly mundane routines.

I was building a career and thought my life was great. No matter how tough a day at the office, I didn't have to be responsible for anyone else. Selfish? Maybe.

I worked hard to get to the top of my career. At age nineteen, I began working at a radio station in Houston. I climbed the ladder to managing the New York City office of Vollmer Public Relations. I sacrificed my personal life to get there. Still, whether my choices were intentional or accidental, my life had a purpose, even with the void of marriage and children.

Then I met Adam, married him at forty, and had a child at forty-three. I had it all. Or so I thought.

In January 2011, Jack was three years old, my father had recently passed away, and I was at a crossroads in my life, especially at work. My boss, Helen, had recently sold her agency, and my hours were reduced to part-time.

Adam and I often discussed how life would look if I stopped working and stayed home to raise Jack. I brought up the subject more than Adam, but he had a lot to say.

"Is it possible for me to quit my job?" I asked Adam one night over dinner. "I'm miserable at work, and it's unfair to my bosses, the agency, and me. And it's certainly not fair to you and Jack."

"If that's what you want to do, we'll make it work. We'll have to budget better," Adam teased.

The b-word only made me consider how I'd pay for my monthly hair color appointments. I'd been coloring my hair since my late twenties, and I certainly wasn't going to stop.

"I'll start my own freelance business and get clients to bring in money and keep funding my hair habit, but I'll work from home to be with Jack. Plenty of individuals and small companies would hire me for my services, right?"

"Of course," he said.

Despite my eagerness to leave my current job, the truth was I did like working; at least, I enjoyed making money to pay for my hair care. Knowing I had a path forward if I chose to take it, I shelved the idea for a few months and continued with the agency.

One morning, while experiencing a typical New York City night-mare work commute of enduring rerouted trains and packed subway cars, then walking in frigid cold weather to my office, I asked myself what I was doing.

Ever since Jack had been born, this question had plagued my thoughts. I either needed to be more honest about the real answer or admit I was in total denial of the actual reason: I didn't want to work anymore and wanted to stay home to raise my child. As Mark Twain is often credited as saying, "Denial ain't just a river in Egypt."

My state of denial meant I did not understand that it would be okay to leave the job that once represented the pinnacle of my success to stay home and raise the child I'd longed to have. Right or wrong, I worried about what it would look like to others if I swapped out one dream for another. But I didn't realize that what others thought didn't matter because the only person who could make me happy was me.

. . .

In February 2011, my team coordinated an event for one of our clients, the Texas state tourism office. I loved working on this account because who better to promote Texas in New York City than a native Texan?

The event to launch a new Texas-inspired nail polish collection from OPI occurred at a swanky midtown salon and spa. The names of the different polishes included: "San Tan-Tonio," "Guy Meets Gal-veston," "It's Totally Fort Worth It," "Austin-tatious Turquoise," and "Houston We Have a Purple."

Fashion and beauty editors sipped wine and ate cheese while getting free manicures and pedicures throughout the evening. Also in attendance was the First Lady of Texas, Anita Perry, whose husband, Governor Rick Perry, was a good friend of my cousins, Fred and Kay.

"Hello, Mrs. Perry. I'm Judy Haveson, from Houston," I said upon meeting the first lady. "You know my cousins, Fred and Kay Zeidman."

"Oh my goodness, I love them! They're good people," she replied.

Fred is politically active, both nationally and locally in Texas. He always tells me to drop his name when appropriate, and what better person to name-drop to than the governor's wife?

"Yes, they are. We're very close; they're godparents to my three-year-old son, Jack."

"How wonderful. How is raising a young child in New York City while having a busy career?"

While I'm sure this was only small talk, it still struck a chord. I froze when considering how to answer Mrs. Perry. I honestly didn't know how to respond.

"I do the best I can," I said.

I'm one of many women to answer the question of how we maintain a work/life balance. I watched all my girlfriends have multiple kids, go back to work, and continue to build careers. They seemed to have it all figured out. But this wasn't about them or anyone else. It was about me. And my girlfriends weren't in their forties when they first had children.

For several months, I went through the motions at work. I sat at my desk each day, and for the first time in my career, I watched the clock.

One day, after another hellish commute to and from work, I came home and informed Adam I wanted to revisit my shelved plan to become a work-from-home mom. We'd had this conversation before, but now I was ready to put the idea into action.

"I'm going to hand my resignation to Helen tomorrow," I told Adam.

"If that's what you want to do, I'll fully support you," he said.

"I'm scared. What if I'm making a mistake?"

"You'll never know until you try," he said.

Having Adam's support gave me the confidence to move forward. The following day, I gave Helen my resignation.

"I'm torn about this decision because I've loved working with you and with everyone these past fourteen years, but my heart isn't in it anymore," I told Helen. "I want to stay home and raise Jack. Of course, I have no idea if I'm making the right decision or not, but I'll never know unless I try."

"Judy, I understand and believe this is the best decision for you right now. You're going to be fine and I'm here for you, always," Helen said.

And to this day, Helen and I are still in touch. She will forever be my mentor and a big part of my life.

After I resigned, I sat alone in my apartment with a toddler, no job, and an uncertain future. Things were looking great! I thought about the advice given to me by my father. He always said, "If that's what you want to do, you can do it." No matter what I wanted in life, he would always tell me that if it was something I wanted to do, big or small, just do it. This simple phrase became my words to live by.

My First Mom Friend

IN 2001, I MOVED to Manhattan. The beauty of moving to New York City in my late thirties, with no husband and no children, was that I instantly connected with a group of successful, career-minded women precisely like me. In Texas, I'd never felt I'd belonged because all my friends were getting married and having children in their twenties and thirties.

But once living in New York City, I wasn't alone in my husbandless situation. I surrounded myself with other women who also had a second job: dating. My single girlfriends and I often shared and compared notes about dating horror stories.

One night I sat with Karen and Renée at a Chinese restaurant on the Upper East Side. Karen and I had met in high school in Houston and thanks to our mutual friend, Ron, we had reconnected when I moved to New York. She introduced me to her friend, Renée. While eating mediocre Chinese food and gossiping about our latest dating disasters, I noticed a familiar guy walk into the restaurant with a girl on his arm.

"Karen, didn't you go out with that guy?" I asked.

"Yes, I did," she said. "He was nice, but not for me. Maybe one of you would like him."

Diplomacy was an art form for Karen; she's an attorney. This was her go-to statement about every man she went out with whom she didn't feel was worthy of a second date.

"Too late," I said. "I've already gone out with that guy and wasn't impressed. And seeing as he chose this cheap Chinese restaurant to take his date to, I doubt Renée is interested either."

Unlike Karen, I had no filter.

"Will we ever find the one?" we'd often ask each other. "Why is dating so hard?"

While we would always be there for each other in our time of dating despair, secretly, we all wanted the same thing: a husband and a family. But we had high standards: a.k.a. we were picky.

"I wonder who will get married first?" Renée asked one night.

I never imagined it would be me.

. . .

Most of my other friends in New York and the surrounding area were married with kids when I walked down the aisle. After Jack was born, my friends' kids were in elementary, middle, and high school, which did not make for great playdates with a newborn. This meant I had to leave my comfort zone and put myself out there, much as I did with dating. But this time, I had to find a new circle of mom friends. And I knew I'd most likely be the oldest.

Finding friends at any age is hard. It's not as if you can walk up to someone and say, "Hi, want to be my friend?" That's how we did it in kindergarten. If you ask this question as an adult, the other person may assume you have a personality disorder.

Fortunately, everyone is on a level playing field when you have an infant and are around other people with newborns and toddlers. But what happens when you're the oldest mom?

Will I be accepted into the world of younger moms? Will I fit in? Will they think I'm too old? Will I think they're too young?

In some ways, being a first-time mother in my forties in New York City meant not feeling alone, even though I was in a city of nearly nine million people. I could see new people daily and build new relationships with other mothers and nannies at the playground, as well as my doormen, diner workers, etc. Yes, you can make these relationships in the suburbs, but in the city, many women looked like I did: a mom in her forties with a little one. I wasn't an anomaly.

While I was among the oldest moms on the playground at age forty-three, others weren't far behind. I met women anywhere from two to five years younger than I was.

Of course, there was still a large group of those up to fifteen years younger, and I loved to shock them when I revealed my actual age. "You're how old?" "I want to see your driver's license; I don't believe you!" "You look amazing, and I hope I look like you in ten years." I heard it all.

Adam and I lived in a large apartment building with forty-eight floors, more than four hundred units, and at least two to three kids in each hallway. When Jack was barely a year old, one of the moms coordinated a social get-together for families in the courtyard of the building.

"Let's go check it out, and who knows, maybe I'll find a new mom friend," I told Adam.

I met a woman with a newborn son eight months younger than Jack. I quickly learned they lived in the apartment located directly above our unit.

"I'm Judy, and we live in 34G," I told her.

"I'm Shira, and we live in 35G," she said. "I hope you don't hear our baby crying."

"I wouldn't be able to hear him over Jack," I assured her.

I learned Shira was Jewish, just a few years younger than I was, and grew up in New York. She was an attorney but no longer practicing. We talked for a while and exchanged numbers to get together. I worked full-time, so my get-together options were limited to after work or weekends. We agreed to stay in touch and went our separate ways. I believed Shira and I could become good friends.

When I eventually left my job, Shira became my first mom friend, and we became very close. Together, we took our sons all over the city, visiting museums, kid-friendly restaurants, and every playground in Central Park. Our wine playdates / gossip sessions were a weekly event, and sometimes multiple times a week.

At the foot of our building sat the New York Kids Club. This space served as a daycare center that Jack attended when he was two. The club occasionally hosted Friday playdates for children and their families and served light snacks and drinks.

One Friday afternoon, when Shira and I took our kids, we noticed the club offered juice boxes for the children and Coronas for the adults.

"What's with the beer? Have you ever seen this before?" Shira asked.

"Well, I am from Texas," I kidded. "No, but after being around these kids all week, I'd need a beer too."

"I doubt anyone will drink a beer here," she said.

And as soon as she said that, one of the dads popped the top off the bottle and started guzzling.

"At least our playdates are more sophisticated with wine," I added.

Jack and Shira's son, Levi, became best buddies, practically brothers, and brought out the silliest in each other. Like our sons, sometimes Shira and I also brought out the most ridiculous in each other.

Shira and I experienced motherhood's best and worst together, and I was always thankful to have her by my side. For example, at the playdate when our sons decided to play barbershop.

"Mom, look what I did to Jack's hair!" Levi proudly exclaimed.

We both stared in shock as a laughing Jack walked out of the bathroom with his hair spiked straight up and out because of the handful of Aquaphor Levi had used as hair gel.

"Oh my gosh!" I said. "How will I ever get this out of Jack's hair?"

"I'll Google it," Shira said.

After an exhaustive search of every article on how to get Aquaphor or Vaseline out of hair and dousing Jack's hair in shampoo, conditioner, and Dawn dish soap, we finally discovered that baby oil did the trick.

"Baby oil worked like magic, and the Aquaphor slid right out of Jack's hair," I told Shira. And his hair had never felt softer.

Another time I was so grateful for Shira's friendship was the afternoon Jack gave himself a concussion.

During an otherwise ordinary playdate at my apartment, Jack and Levi destroyed Jack's bedroom by pulling his toys and a stack of Berenstain Bears books off the bookshelves. A few of the books' covers ripped and Shira helped me tape them back together. As we sat repairing the books in the living room, Jack and Levi ran in and started jumping around us.

"Did I just see the lamp move?" Shira asked. "I think Jack hit his head on the table."

"I'm not sure. Jack, are you okay?"

At that moment, I pulled Jack closer to look at him, and he threw up all over the place. It didn't appear to be your typical stomach-bug mess; it was bright red. Shira and I panicked.

"Oh my gosh, he's throwing up blood!" I screamed. And I quickly scooped Jack up to get him off my beautiful Oriental rug and away from the furniture. He kept throwing up once I got him into the bathroom, and it looked like a scene from *Law & Order*. The walls were stained red from his projectile vomit.

While Shira and I freaked out, poor traumatized Levi yelled, "Mommy, I want to go home!"

"Levi, I have to stay and help Judy. I promise we'll go home soon," she told him.

I quickly called the doctor to let her know what happened.

"I think he hit his head on the end table, and he's throwing up blood," I told the doctor.

"You need to bring him to the ER to ensure he doesn't have a brain bleed," she told me. "I'll call ahead so you won't have to wait."

The urgency of this event centered on Jack's hemophilia. While he has mild hemophilia, not moderate or severe, he's still at risk for bleeding episodes, primarily internal.

"We're not concerned with cuts and scrapes as much as internal bleeds," the doctor always told us. "It's not what you can see; it's what you can't see."

And this was the exact scenario we were faced with now.

Knowing it would be faster to drive in our car to the hospital instead of hailing a taxi during rush hour, I called Adam while he was driving home from work.

"Are you almost home?" I asked Adam.

"Yes, I'm a few blocks away," he replied.

"I'll explain when I'm in the car but meet us in front of the apartment. We need to take Jack to the ER," I told him.

I quickly ran around the apartment gathering Jack's things as I didn't know how long we'd be at the hospital.

Before I left, Shira and I cleaned Jack's mess to ensure no stains remained on my rug. Upon further inspection, I noticed what appeared to be berry chunks.

"Jack, what did you have as a snack at school today?" I asked him.

"Berry parfait," he said.

Then Shira and I started laughing and couldn't stop. This wasn't blood; it was berry parfait! While Shira and I were temporarily relieved by this discovery, poor Levi was still upset. I think today, he still has PTSD from the incident.

Knowing this information lowered my blood pressure, but we still took Jack to the ER. In the end, he had a slight concussion from hitting his head on the table. But regardless of how frightened I was during the ordeal, having Shira by my side helped calm me down.

Jack and Levi went on to attend different schools, and we moved out of the building. Still, they remain good friends, or, as they say, "brothers." While they don't see each other as often as they did as kids, their mischievousness when together is as strong as when they were four, maybe more. Same for Shira and me. No matter our circumstances, Shira will always be my first partner in motherhood and forever friend.

Stop Me Before I Volunteer Again

IF I LEARNED ANYTHING from my girlfriends with children, getting involved in school activities is the fastest way to make mom friends. When Jack started at Woodside Preschool, I immediately became a class representative. I told myself I'd take a break when he got to kindergarten, but I didn't listen to myself and got lured back into the mix. My role in the Parents' Association (PA) continued through sixth grade. I proudly volunteered to coordinate, participate in, decorate, and set up class parties, book fairs, uniform sales, food festivals, and more.

While I took my rep role seriously and loved being an insider to the school (which allowed me to keep tabs on Jack's progress), it wasn't a job. However, many women treated their position as one. Also, none of my friends warned me that once you get sucked into the endless parade of coordination, planning, and parties, it's hard to quit and usually leaves you screaming, "Please stop me before I volunteer again!"

For the kindergarten class party, my co-rep volunteered to host the get-together at her apartment.

"I've been a class rep for many years with my older daughter, so planning this soiree is easy," she told me. "I'll hire the caterer I've used in the past to provide all the food, and you can just write me a check for your portion."

I didn't realize the class party would be a catered event. In my mind, we'd ask other parents to bring food or wine, sit around talking for a few hours, and call it a night.

"I've ordered a variety of cheese and meat platters, salads, baby lamb chops, sliders, pigs in a blanket, fruit, crudités, and dessert," she said. "Your portion is $350."

And she said all of this with a straight face.

Who knew how expensive being a class rep would be? What did I sign up for?

And it didn't stop with the caterer. We also ordered glassware, plates and utensils, decorations, and coordinated the Paperless Post, making this small affair feel more like a bar mitzvah than a gathering of kindergarten parents.

The party was a roaring success, and everyone had a great time. Of course, it also helped that my co-rep lived in a beautifully decorated full-floor apartment overlooking the Hudson River, with the most oversized Manhattan kitchen I'd ever seen. The kitchen included a huge center island with space around it for people to gather.

Despite the party's success, I found myself rethinking my PA involvement. Would every class party be like this one? Was this what the parents at this school expected? Did I want to be this involved? I now understood why "working" moms never volunteered. Perhaps I should return to work so I wouldn't have to be a class rep?

Because I "represented" the class, I also became a sounding board for many disgruntled parents as they complained about everything from homework to lunch choices. Having worked in the public relations service business for many years, I began comparing uptight parents to angry clients. This theory made sense to me because we paid the equivalent of a high retainer fee in school tuition.

One of the moms I met through the PA was Meridith. She had three children: a daughter two years older than Jack and twin boys one year younger. Meridith was Jewish and only a few years younger than I was. We had much in common and instantly connected over our shared generational interests and motherhood experiences.

Of course, unbeknownst to me, she became aware of me long before we met. One day, while attending a PA meeting, she approached me and said, "I've already decided you'll be perfect for the PA board."

"Why me?" I asked her.

"Because I like you, and I know we'd have fun together," she said.

I took that as a compliment.

Meridith also lived close to me, and we'd often commute to and from school in the mornings with our kids.

"I'm not sure what I'd do without our morning chat sessions," I told her one morning on the bus. "We seem to solve all the world's problems on this short commute, and it's the best part of my day."

Being on the PA board was sometimes challenging. Still, it helped solidify friendships with Meredith and the other great women I'd otherwise not have met.

Another great aspect about making mom friends in New York City was how many women who were now stay-at-home moms came from different career backgrounds. I was surrounded by former bankers, lawyers, accountants, financial executives, and more. We all had these great careers and had decided to pause to raise our children. We were still determining whether this would be a good idea, but sharing the experience with like-minded women made it more bearable and enjoyable. But once again, I remained the oldest mom.

While being older didn't bother me too much, I occasionally wished I hadn't waited so long to have a child. I worried that Jack would resent having older parents when his friends' parents were so much younger. Of course, this projection was only in my head because once I became friends with younger moms and they found out how much older I was, they never believed me. In those moments, I thanked my mother for passing on her youthful genes.

. . .

One afternoon at Jack's swim lesson, I met a woman named Julie. Her two daughters had their lessons right before Jack's. I noticed one of the girl's backpacks had the Dwight School logo, the school Jack attended.

"Do your girls go to Dwight?" I asked the woman sitting next to me. "My son goes there and is in kindergarten."

"Yes, Ava is in first grade, and Kira is in pre-K," said Julie.

Each week during the kids' swim lessons, Julie and I bonded and gossiped like high school besties while the kids swam, and we barely watched the instruction. Ava and Kira loved Jack and treated him like their brother.

"I don't want to go to swim lessons today!" all three kids would say with a whine each week.

"You're going," Julie and I always told them. But if one of them missed a lesson, they all skipped—three peas in a pod.

Julie and I wanted them to learn to swim, but truthfully, we looked forward to hanging out with each other more.

One afternoon, on the way home, Jack decided to play a trick and show off for the girls. Kira was being pushed in her stroller by Julie, and Ava and Jack were on their scooters. Jack attempted a stunt that ended up with his scooter speeding down a massive hill, right into the oncoming traffic.

"Oh no!" Jack and the girls yelled.

"This can't end well," I said to Julie, praying no one would run over the scooter.

When we got to the bottom of the hill, the scooter sat perfectly still, right side up, in the middle of the road. Cars dodged and swerved around it. We all still laugh about it today.

As our children bonded over swimming and scooter tricks, Julie and I connected through babysitter and nanny nightmares, hair color appointments, keratin treatments, school events, and life. Together, we attended countless cocktail parties and school gatherings.

During one of our chat sessions at the pool, I mentioned I had a milestone birthday coming up during the summer.

"We'll all turn forty eventually," Julie said.

"You think I'm turning forty?" I asked her. "I'm turning fifty!"

"There's no way that's possible," she replied. "You look like you're in your thirties."

I loved Julie before, but I now knew I'd always love her.

When the instructor at the health club where the kids took lessons got fired, management tried, but failed, to find another teacher. We vowed to keep them together.

"We have to find a new place that will take all three kids for swim lessons," Julie said.

"Of course," I said. "We can't break up the 'three musketeers,' and we can't lose our weekly chat sessions."

Fortunately, we found another health club close to our apartment buildings and the kids continued lessons and Julie and I our gossip sessions. While swim lessons and school had brought Julie and me together, I was confident our families would remain close far beyond these activities.

In addition to volunteering for and attending school activities, the moms often got together to drink. Several years later, at an end-of-year school celebration, a group of fourth-grade moms descended upon Tavern on the Green, an iconic New York City Central Park restaurant. That evening, drinks flowed freely under a beautiful early summer sky. And then the bill arrived.

"Am I reading this right?" I asked Danny, one of the fourth-grade moms. "Did we drink twenty bottles of rosé?"

"Oh my gosh, we did," she said. "This is crazy."

After we settled the hefty bill, Tiki, Nuala, Kathryn, and I stayed back to keep drinking. We noticed a twenty-dollar bill on the table from one of the moms who came late to the celebration. She had placed it there to cover her portion of the bill.

"Oh, look, we have more money to keep drinking," said Tiki.

We used the money to order another round of drinks, but soon after, the waiter asked us to leave.

"We're closing now, so no more drinks," he said.

"What do you mean?" Kathryn asked. "Are you closing and kicking us out?"

"I'm afraid we are," he replied.

"Let's keep going then," said Nuala.

These ladies, all younger than I was, knew how to drink.

Adam was out of town on business, and Jack was with a babysitter. It was getting late, and I'd had enough to drink. I was tired and wanted to go home.

"I'm going home to relieve the babysitter," I told them.

"No, you can't leave us!" they said. "We need to keep going."

"Wow, do y'all have hollow legs or what?" I asked. "You girls go on. I'm out."

One of Kathryn's sandals broke as we walked away from Central Park.

"Oh no, my bloody shoe broke," she said in her British accent, slurring the words. "I can't walk."

"Here, take my shoes," I told her. "I live down the block and don't have much further to walk."

I took off my shoes and gave them to Kathryn. Feeling no pain, I didn't let walking on the filthy streets of New York City worry me or my feet. I couldn't wait to get home and shower.

As I crossed over Broadway on my way home, barefoot, I heard my name.

"Judy, we decided to come to your apartment instead of continuing to another bar," they yelled. "Wait for us!"

I waited for the girls to cross Broadway safely.

"I guess the bar you walked into took one look and asked you to leave," I kidded.

We stumbled into my building under the staring eyes of my doorman.

"You ladies look like you're having a good time tonight," Esad said.

"Yes, we are, but don't tell Adam!" I said.

After I paid the babysitter, we opened another bottle of wine. I'd lost count but believed we were up to twenty-two bottles. Jack was asleep in his room.

"Shhh," I said. "We can't wake up Jack."

Kathryn didn't hear me because she turned up the music as we continued drinking, and we started singing and dancing to One Direction in my living room. Suddenly we saw Jack walking out of his bedroom, rubbing his eyes. He looked at us with confusion.

"Mommy, why are you having a PA meeting in the middle of the night?" he asked.

We all started laughing. Poor Jack.

Finally, we called it a night. Tiki and Nuala went home together, and because Kathryn lived in another direction, we called her a separate Uber. Her apartment was on West 85th Street, but because we were slightly visually impaired from all the wine, we accidently put East 85th Street into the Uber app. Thankfully, Kathryn noticed before her Uber driver took her on a joyride through the city.

After this one night, it no longer mattered that I was the oldest mom on the playground. I was part of an incredible group of women who didn't care what age my driver's license indicated. But one thing I knew for sure: I could no longer drink as I did in my twenties, thirties, and forties. I'm still recovering from that hangover.

Fifty Shades of Fifty and the Fountain of Youth

THE BEST PART OF having a child in your forties is being friends with women who have paved the way to motherhood for you. They're there to help you troubleshoot, lend a hand, and even whisk you away to an island to get you drunk.

I met Hannah when she was twenty-one and I was nine-teen. Hannah is more than a friend. She's my soul sister and partner in crime. In our younger days, we were always the life of the party and often scammed our way to fun. As we got older, the good times continued, with a little more caution. For her fiftieth birthday, she gathered a group of girlfriends in the Bahamas for an unforgettable celebration.

The getaway marked the first time I left my four-year-old son, Jack, and husband, Adam, at home to fend for themselves. Of course, preparing for this journey came with weeks, even months, of planning, and I'm not talking about for the actual trip.

From arranging babysitters, packing lunches for camp, leaving paint-by-number instructions, and mapping out ideas and possible activities, I was exhausted before I got on the plane. But it was all worth it to join fourteen women, many of whom I didn't know, to celebrate Hannah.

The average age on this trip was probably around forty-six. Not for nothing, if anyone looked a day over thirty-five, I was stretching. What is it about aging women today? Women in their forties and fifties now look better than ever. Of course, that's because when we were in our twenties and thirties, we had terrible hairstyles and fashion. Can you say perms and shoulder pads? Please don't let anything from the eighties and nineties come back—ever! Regardless, not being the oldest mom on this trip felt great.

I was the only one with a child under five on the trip, however, which explained why all the other women appeared much younger and more alert than I did. Most of them had kids in high school, and many had children in college. They were nostalgic for years gone by.

"I miss the early years with my children," many said.

"Really? Did you forget about a four-year-old who constantly whines and throws temper tantrums when he doesn't get his way?"

"Well, maybe not that," they said.

"Do you long for the days of emotional outbursts for no reason or for the feeling of never finishing a single thought because your child has his mouth in constant motion and never stops talking?" I continued.

"Okay, no," they said. "But one day, you'll miss it too. Wait until he starts applying to college."

They had a valid point, but I got mine across.

We experienced four glorious days in the hot Bimini sun, including lying by the pool and beach daily, enjoying frozen rum drinks, and holding a mock wedding where I "married" Jill, the Catholic beauty. Jill wore Carmen's bra as a yarmulke, and I wore Susie's white sundress as we stood under the chuppah exchanging our vows. Jill almost broke the glass in her bare feet (okay, we didn't get married, but we did have a lot of frozen piña coladas!).

However, the most memorable part of the weekend was a trip to the Healing Hole. If this trip was our Fifty Shades of Fifty, this excursion was our Red Playroom of Pain.

I'm no stranger to good marketing copy and have even written some in my day. But rarely have I fallen victim to the allure of words. You know, it's usually hard to bullshit a bullshitter. The copy: "For decades, the Healing Hole at Bimini claims to have therapeutic properties and rejuvenating power. Dip yourself in this spring and find its benefits while enjoying the peace and beauty of this place on earth. Ask for the Healing Hole option to dip your body in this legendary spring."

The brochure failed to mention kayaking through mangroves to get to the hole. The round trip lasted three hours, and we rowed six miles. Kayaking? Really? There's a reason I never got that badge in Girl Scouts. Furthermore, why do they make it look so easy on *Dora the Explorer?*

We went two-by-two in our kayaks (except for Kim, the one brave woman who went solo) for much longer than three hours. And you know everyone was singing the theme to *Gilligan's Island*.

Whenever we asked our guides if we had arrived yet, they responded with "Oh, we're about sixty percent of the way there." We were 60 percent of the way there the whole damn trip.

My kayak partner, Carmen, and I kept getting stuck in the mangroves because we were never in sync. We were, essentially, going in circles. We were the last to make it to the hole. And wouldn't you know it, something stung me the minute we arrived at the spot. Not surprising, seeing as I saw hundreds of jellyfish floating in the water on the way there. It was like *Survivor* along the Caribbean.

All the girls got out to experience the hole, but I passed.

"Judy, don't be lame. Leave the kayak and get over to the hole," Carmen and the others yelled at me.

"I'm good, thanks," I replied.

"Don't you want to be healed?" they said.

"Judging by the jungle vines and bugs swarming the area, this isn't my idea of healing," I replied. "I'd rather heal in a spa."

As it turned out, I was the smart one by passing on the hole. The therapeutic attraction with its mosquitos and other swamp-like creatures was anything but healing.

"Who's lame now?" I asked the girls as they swam back to their kayaks, swatting beetles, cicadas, and other island species away.

On the way back, the "rescue" boat kept coming by to ask if we wanted to get on board.

"You ladies look like you want to give up," the rescue boat driver said. "Come on board, and we'll take you the rest of the way."

"Are you crazy?" we responded. "Do you seriously think we'd surrender to your rescue after kayaking this far?"

Little did they know, we'd have quit in a minute if no one would have seen us. But at least after three hours and six miles of kayaking, I didn't have to feel guilty about all those piña coladas I drank and the lack of exercise all weekend.

Bimini also boasts being home to the Fountain of Youth. We stopped to see it on our way to the resort. Of course, when we got out to experience the fountain's youthful essence and possibly drink from it, the driver screamed, "Don't touch the water!" His warning probably concerned the rusty bucket hanging from the monument.

The trip was fantastic, and I loved being part of this group of rock-star women celebrating our extraordinary friend, Hannah. But I was so excited to return home to my husband and my whining, temper-tantrum-throwing, nonstop-talking four-year-old. I knew it was a matter of time before I'd be nostalgic for these days too.

The Zen of Spin

THE SUMMER I TURNED fifty, indoor cycling became the latest fitness craze in New York City. At the time, Peloton barely existed except in shopping mall showrooms. Soul Cycle studios started popping up all over Manhattan. While many of my friends flocked to Soul because of the party, cult-like environment, I stayed away, think-ing I'd never get through one class without passing out or throwing up.

Then, FlyWheel, a new indoor cycling company, opened a studio in my neighborhood, directly across the street from my apartment. My gym had spin classes and I'd always wondered what they were like.

During workout sessions with Jenny, my trainer, I remember laughing at the over-caffeinated, hyped-up instructors barking orders at riders. The loudest and most annoying heavy-base music that shook the floor was always playing during these classes.

"Why must these instructors scream?" I asked Jenny. "I'm all for being motivated, especially regarding exercise, but they're like army drill sergeants yelling at recruits."

She laughed and said, "Stick to weight training. It's better for you."

But there had to be a reason the spin craze was taking off and studios were popping up all over the city like Starbucks.

Adam has always been a fitness enthusiast. His journey began during college when he trained to be a reserve in the LAPD. He'd often tell me about his different exercise programs, including spinning.

"Spinning has been around since the eighties," Adam said. "It's one of the fastest ways to burn six hundred to seven hundred calories a ride."

"Well, I'm sure that's still true, but in the eighties, I bet taking one class didn't cost thirty-six dollars," I said.

There is nothing like throwing a bunch of stationary exercise bikes into a dark studio and turning them into cash cows.

. . .

One day, Sarah, Jack's rock-star babysitter at the time, told me she tried a FlyWheel class at the studio across the street from my apartment.

"You have to come to a class with me and try it. You'll love it!" she said a little too enthusiastically.

It's important to note that Sarah is half my age, a half foot taller, and has no body fat on her, anywhere. Of course, she loved it. To her, it was like, well, riding a bike.

If not for the fact that the front door to the studio sat a hundred feet from my building, I probably wouldn't have stepped foot inside FlyWheel. Still, because of the convenience, and that I would have a buddy there to resuscitate me when I inevitably passed out, I decided to give it a go.

My first Fly class was anything but easy, and I was sure it would be my last class. I huffed and puffed through forty-five minutes of vigorous riding (and loud music). If not for the shoe clips keeping me firmly attached to the bike like super glue, I'm convinced I would have flown over the handlebars and landed on the instructor.

Riding next to Sarah was stressful. Her long, lean legs glided smoothly with each pedal stroke, and she barely broke a sweat. She looked like she could keep riding for hours after the class ended.

"You make it look so easy," I told her.

"Are you kidding? I could barely get through class," she said.

"Well, it didn't look that way to me."

Everything is wasted on the youth.

Even though I was in a cool, dark room where other riders couldn't see me, much less care I was there, it may as well have been Moab as I had never sweat so much in such a short period as I did during that one spin class. No surprise, seeing as I burned more calories in forty-five minutes than I had probably burned in a month.

I was dead. I could barely walk. I couldn't sit down. I felt every bit of my almost fifty years. But strangely, I wanted to go back. It was awesome, minus the inability to walk or sit down. And I never looked back.

Spinning quickly became my obsession. Some days, I had great rides; others, the classes challenged my existence. And I eventually scrapped the padded cycle shorts. The music was loud, but I barely heard it. The teachers were fantastic and motivating but not annoying. As a big bonus, it's always exciting when a celebrity like Sting comes to class and rides on the bike next to you.

I also became friends with many FlyWheel instructors, including Wendy, Megan, Amanda, Albert, and Brian. They were the true motivators and made class bearable, and I loved it when they gave me a shout-out during class. Of course, they were probably calling my name out loud to make sure I hadn't passed out.

The FlyWheel leaderboard allowed riders to compete against others in the class for bragging rights, but I never put my name up there. Partly because the only person I competed against was myself. Also, I didn't want to embarrass myself, knowing I'd land at the bottom of the pack. I quickly learned to ignore that one rider that outpaced everyone as if they were competing in the Tour de France.

After the COVID pandemic, FlyWheel went out of business. Soul Cycle was sold to Equinox, a prominent health company. We eventually bought a Peloton bike for our house. I quickly became obsessed with it.

While I sometimes miss the excitement and energy of taking a live in-studio class, surrounded by other riders and a fun instructor to motivate me, I love going at my own pace in the comfort of my home.

And to think it took Jack's babysitter, Sarah, to convince me to take that first spin class.

"Did you think I'd return after that first class?" I asked Sarah several years later. "I truly thought I'd die that day."

"I told you that you'd love it," she said. "Now, you make it look easy to me."

As strange as this sounds, spin is my Zen. While Zen is typically associated with a more reflective exercise such as yoga, you'd be surprised at the calmness you can experience once you clip in and hit your groove. Your heart races, your legs spin at a hundred rpms, and sweat pours down your face. For me, the exertion cleared and eased my mind. Because, like how I view life and parenthood, it's all about the journey.

Fifty Life Lessons at Fifty

THE DAY I TURNED fifty, I thought, *Wow, that's a big, ginormous number, and I have a six-year-old son!* I remembered being in high school and calculating how old I'd be in 2000 (thirty-six for those who aren't fast with math). I also remembered thinking thirty-six was a gigantic number and figured I'd be married with children by then. It's funny how quickly that thinking changed.

While many of my friends struggled with turning fifty, I marked the milestone with a sense of pride, some nostalgia, and a big sigh of relief that I had lived long enough to enjoy life, get married to a wonderful man, and, yes, have a child, even if that event came toward the latter part of my first fifty years.

I spent the day reflecting about all the life lessons I'd learned over the past half century. I also considered whether I'd ever make it to Smucker's 100th Birthday celebration list. However, did I really want to be on that list?

Here are fifty life lessons I've learned over the past fifty years (in no particular order):

1. Use your filter before speaking (still working on this one!).
2. There are many things in life you can't change but your hair color is not one of them (thanks, Mom!).

3. Conquer your fears and try to do something out of your comfort zone, unless it will land you in jail or on *America's Most Wanted*.

4. Perception is often not reality.

5. Self-fulfilling prophecies usually come true, especially if they're negative.

6. Perms are generally a bad idea.

7. Women should understand and play at least one sport.

8. Love may mean never having to say you're sorry, but if you really piss off a loved one, tell them you're sorry.

9. NEVER say *never*.

10. Being a late bloomer has its advantages.

11. The most essential accessory you should always wear is a smile.

12. Be a positive example to young, impressionable minds—especially your children—who watch and learn from you.

13. Learn how to do something in the kitchen, even if it's boiling water.

14. Visit as many states and countries as possible in your lifetime.

15. Stay in touch with friends from childhood; they will always remind you of the person you were and the person you wanted to become, if you're not there yet.

16. You can choose your friends, unlike your relatives.

17. Appreciate your parents daily, even if they're no longer here. You'll understand why once you're a parent.

18. Pay your taxes. And your parking tickets.

19. Be on a jury. It's a fascinating process but do pray your fate won't rely on it one day.

20. Don't drink and drive (and today, add texting); it's not worth it.

21. Failure is not a sign of weakness; just fail fast and don't make the same mistakes twice.

22. Send a thank-you note when someone does something nice for you.

23. If given the opportunity, move out of your hometown. You can go home again if you want to.

24. Bad fashion styles from the seventies and eighties are still wrong when they come back around (can you say bell bottoms and shoulder pads?).

25. Go to at least one major sporting event in your lifetime.

26. We all have angels in heaven; some even share our birthdays.

27. There are two types of people in the world: those who know and those who want to know. Be the one who knows, but don't be a know-it-all.

28. If you have nothing nice to say, tell your best friend because they'll probably think it's funny.

29. Big boobs will get you free drinks (I'm not proud; well, sort of).

30. NOTHING IS EASY!

31. Your life will be tested repeatedly, and you'll only know your strength once you must use it.

32. Wearing white before Easter and after Labor Day is okay.

33. Take responsibility for your actions, and don't pass blame for something you did in the first place.

34. Things typically happen for a reason, and if you can't figure out why, the reason is probably not yours to understand.

35. Life is what happens when you're busy making plans.

36. Mother–daughter relationships are complicated.

37. Bad things can and do happen to good people.

38. The only thing constant in life is change. Embrace it.

39. You're never too old to reinvent yourself.

40. God's last name is not dammit (something I thought it was my entire childhood).

41. Hug, kiss, and tell your kids and spouse/partner you love them daily.

42. It's not who you are, it's what you wear. No one really cares who you are, but people always notice what you're wearing.

43. Indulge in some sort of extravagance at least once a year. You deserve it.

44. Karma is a bitch and things do come back around.

45. Respect your elders. They've been around the block a time or two, and you can probably learn something from them.

46. Give up your seat on a bus or subway to someone who needs it more than you.

47. A child's laughter will always make you smile.

48. Don't become a jack-of-all-trades, master of none. Pick a lane.

49. Tell the truth but learn the art of diplomacy.

50. Carpe diem!

Here's to the next fifty and learning more along the way!

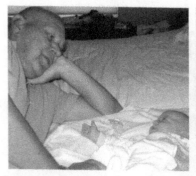

Photo Captions

Through the Years
> Adam & Judy Dating
> The Bride & Groom
> The Expecting Parents
> Babymoon in Anguilla
> The Cohen Family

Family
> Papa & Jack
> Grammy & Jack
> With my parents
> Grammy & Papa at Jack's 1st Birthday
> Jack with his entire family: Grandpa Harry, Aunt Lisa, Grammy & Papa, Mom & Dad

I'm a Mom!
> The minute my life changed forever
> Multi-tasking on maternity leave
> When the nanny gets sick
> Bring your child to work day

The City Kid
> Sitting with Manuel at the counter at Old John's
> Jack in Central Park
> Riding bikes with dad in Central Park
> Subway adventure on the 7 Train

Jack's Harem

    Jack and Desiree

    Jack and Kelly

    Jack and Lizzie on set of ABC11-Raleigh-Durham

    Jack and Sidney

    Jack and Sarah

My Go-to Mom Experts

    Jack with Melinda (and Mimi!)

    Jack with Godmother Kay

    Jack with Hannah

    Jack with Carmen

The Bar Mitzvah & The Dog

    Jack reading from the Torah

    My b'nei mitzvah partner

    I finally get a dog!

    Toby – the best dog ever!

Today, I Am a Woman, Albeit Forty - three Years Later

IN THE SUMMER OF 1977, I turned thirteen with a mouth full of braces and a head of feathered hair. Fleetwood Mac's "Rumors" and the Eagles' "Hotel California" ruled the radio. I was a "Dancing Queen," or so I thought. Most of my Jewish friends had already celebrated or prepared for their bar and bat mitzvahs.

Not me.

Instead, I sat on the sidelines as a guest at many clubhouses, country clubs, and roller rinks. I didn't mind not attending Hebrew school, with all that studying and tutoring, but I felt a little left out. I'm sure my friends thought I was lucky not to have to endure it; the grass is always greener. But I still wondered what could have been, and I had regrets.

Bat mitzvah translates to "daughter of the commandments" and is based on the ritual of the bar mitzvah, which translates to "son of the commandments." The ceremony signifies a young woman or man who reaches adulthood under Jewish law, typically at thirteen. Each is called to the Torah to read passages and recite prayers. But this ritual hasn't always been equal.

For girls, the rite of passage was used only to celebrate maturity, not to participate equally in reading from the Torah, like their male counterpart. This suppressed ideal mainly existed in Orthodox Judaism but was widely accepted in the Reform, Conservative, and Reconstructionist arms.

My mother, raised as an Orthodox Jew, didn't have a bat mitzvah. This meant my older sister, Celia, and I didn't either. You do what you know.

"I couldn't become a bat mitzvah at age thirteen, even though I attended religious school," my mother told me. "I always felt I missed out as this was something I wanted to accomplish."

Fortunately, this antiquated thinking has diminished through the years, and more and more adult women who were denied the privilege of being called to the Torah are celebrating this rite of passage, including my mother. While visiting Israel with my father in 2000, my mom became a bat mitzvah at age sixty-five.

. . .

In the summer of 2019, when Jack was eleven, we started talking about his upcoming bar mitzvah, which was set for December 2020. Competition is stiff in New York City, so arranging a date years before the ceremony is typical. Of course, when the date was set, it seemed very far away until we received the official bar mitzvah package in the mail. It rivaled a college acceptance packet.

While Adam and I were beyond excited for Jack to reach this milestone, Jack had other ideas. To know Jack is to understand he's a very crafty and determined young man. He had much to say when it came time to discuss bar mitzvah plans.

"I don't want a bar mitzvah," Jack declared one night over dinner.

He'd been a regular at religious school every Sunday morning since kindergarten, so this statement came out of left field to Adam and me.

"Why?" I said, pressing him for an answer.

"No real reason," he said. "I just don't want to have one."

Not the best answer or explanation.

Jack became adamant in his decision, but I thought two could play his game, so I was unwavering as well.

"Having a bar mitzvah isn't negotiable," I said.

So began a series of conversations known as we're-not-going-to-talk-about-not-having-a-bar-mitzvah-today. This series continued for several months.

A bar mitzvah is a generational coming-of-age celebration. My father, who I would never have characterized as a religious man, even had one, albeit with the shortest Haftarah reading (Bible passage from the Torah) on record, or so he always told me. Adam had one as well, so naturally, we would carry on the tradition with Jack.

I didn't want this moment to pass any of us by. Also, I didn't want Jack to sit on the sidelines and have regrets like I did about missing this milestone.

Even though I told Jack his bar mitzvah was non-negotiable, he challenged me.

"Okay, I'll have a bar mitzvah, but on one condition," he said. "I'll do it if you have a bat mitzvah with me."

After letting his request sink in, I pressed him on this colossal condition he bestowed on me.

"Are you sure you want me to do this with you?" I asked him while panicking at the mere thought.

"Mom, you never had a bat mitzvah, and I think it would be cool if we did it together," he explained.

I couldn't believe that I would become a bat mitzvah at age fifty-six, standing beside my son, and that he wanted me to. And to think I thought having a child in my forties made me a late bloomer. After I agreed, I contacted Rabbi Kahn at Temple Emanu-El, our place of worship in New York City.

"Rabbi Kahn, Jack has asked that I become a bat mitzvah when he has his ceremony, making it a b'nei mitzvah," I said. "Is this even possible?"

"Oh, how wonderful, Judy," he said. "It's absolutely possible, and I'm thrilled for you both."

Now, the real fun began.

"Since I never attended Hebrew school, I never learned the language," I told the rabbi. "Do you know an adult Hebrew tutor who can teach me fast?"

"I have the perfect person," he said. "Cantor Jonathan Comisar is wonderful and is already teaching Jack."

I met with Cantor Comisar each week to help prepare my Torah portion and teach me Hebrew. Trust me, the saying "you can't teach an old dog new tricks" proved remarkably accurate.

"Do you think I'll be ready by December fifth?" I asked the cantor.

"I do," he told me. "You're a quick study, and you'll do fine."

Cantor Comisar worked miracles by helping me master Hebrew letters and phrases. After six months, I'd memorized my Torah portion and all the service prayers.

During this same time, I managed to plan a bar mitzvah party at Hill Country, our favorite Texas BBQ restaurant in New York City, coordinate a hotel for all our out-of-town guests, and send out invitations. Everything was going to be perfect.

Then COVID-19 happened. Everyone's COVID story is unique, but one universal aspect that touched us all was the cancellation of milestone events. Whether celebrating a birthday or graduation, welcoming the birth of a new baby, conducting wedding ceremonies, or any other special occasion, we moved everything online or conducted a drive-by to celebrate and show support.

Our b'nei mitzvah (a bar mitzvah and bat mitzvah celebrated together) was scheduled for Saturday, December 5, 2020. As each month of the pandemic ticked off, and nothing appeared normal, we finally decided to do what so many other families had to do with their scheduled events: we moved the ceremony online.

To maintain our momentum, Jack and I continued our tutoring online each week, me with Cantor Comisar and Jack with his Hebrew class.

It would have been easy to get angry at the world for ruining this special moment for Jack, me, and our family and friends, but that's wasted energy. Instead, we rallied everyone to join us on livestream.

Temple Emanu-El in New York City is one of the largest synagogues in the world, with a main sanctuary holding about twenty-five hundred people. Fortunately, the temple allowed us to invite a handful of friends and family to join in person.

Besides Rabbi Kahn, we were joined in person by Cantor Anderson, my mother, who traveled from Florida, and our close friends and their son from our apartment building. In our masks, we all spread out in the first several rows of the palatial sanctuary. Everyone else watched from their living rooms and probably in their pj's.

A prayer called an aliya is read before and after each Torah reading. In a ceremony not conducted during a pandemic, people given the honor of aliya come up on the bimah (stage) to recite the prayer.

My mother and Adam had one aliya, and my cousins and Jack's godparents, Kay and Fred, had the other. While my mother and Adam stood from their seats to give their aliya, Kay and Fred appeared on a screen inside the temple via livestream. Even though I'd rather they been there in person, it brought me great comfort knowing they were in the room.

Things happen for a reason, or so they say. And while I'm still trying to figure out why the COVID pandemic hit the world, in some ways, having this celebration online wasn't the worst outcome.

From behind a plexiglass screen, Jack performed his prayers and Torah portion flawlessly and demonstrated maturity and poise as he gave his speech.

Me? I didn't throw up, something I thought might happen. And while my voice cracked twice, once when I gave my speech to Jack and once when I started to read my Torah portion, making me sound like a thirteen-year-old whose voice was changing, I did it! I could now declare, "Today, I am a woman," albeit forty-three years later. It was a fantastic experience, and I was proud of myself, and Jack.

In addition to reciting prayers and my Torah portion in Hebrew, my other responsibilities for the ceremony included writing a speech to give to Jack. I became emotional when giving the speech, something I didn't anticipate.

Wow! What a journey this has been. I realize today was not how any of us envisioned your bar mitzvah, but in no way does it take away from how hard you've worked for this day. Whether or not you are physically surrounded by family and friends today, they are all with you in spirit (and virtually) and very proud of you.

While I've always been amazed and proud of all your accomplishments, I have newfound pride for all you've learned to become a bar mitzvah, based on my short journey to become a bat mitzvah. I now understand why these milestones happen early on in life, mainly due to not having to wear reading glasses to see the Torah!

It's been so special to share this experience with you, and I'll forever be grateful that you asked me to be your partner. I've learned so much from you, and not just that, you are way better at reading Hebrew and the Torah than I am. And through this process, I hope you have learned some things from me.

If I can pass anything on to you about what it means to be a Jew, it's this: Religion is deeply personal and unique for everyone, and I hope you will experience Judaism in how it makes the most sense to you. For me, being Jewish has always been about faith, family, and tradition. You can add in food too. Enjoy the journey.

Two traditions that are very symbolic today are your tallis and your name.

Today, we present you with your tallis, a prayer shawl and symbol of being wrapped in mitzvot as you begin your journey into Jewish adulthood. But this tallis has an even more special meaning for you.

First, it's a gift from your Grammy, who has been living for this day, even before the thought of you existed. Second, two of the tassels are from my father's tallis. You were just three years old when he passed away. Even though that was nowhere near enough time for you to be together, I know how proud he was of you and how proud he'd be of you today. I can only imagine the trouble you would have gotten into together! I know he's watching over all of us today. Now, he will always be with you too.

The other tradition is your name.

Your father gave me the great honor of choosing your name from my family, and the minute we found out you were going to be a boy, I knew your name would be Jack.

Your great-grandfather was one of the most important male figures in my life and one who taught me so much about being Jewish. He was strong, handsome, independent, funny, loving, generous, stubborn, and compassionate. Funny, that sounds just like you. He would have loved you more than you will ever understand, and you would have loved him too.

Jack, you are a fantastic son, grandson, friend, and person with many unique gifts to give the world. I cannot wait to see what lies ahead for you. The first time I looked at you, I knew I'd met my match. No matter where the road forward takes you in life, I'll forever be with you, cheering you on. And as Grammy always prayed that when I had a child, they should be just like me, you, my son, have not disappointed, and then some. And today, I give you that same wish.

May God always give you the courage to follow your dreams and the strength to follow your heart, allowing you to do the things that make you happy, make the world a better place, and be the best person I know you can be. I love you.

My mother handed me a tissue after I returned to my seat. I'm unsure if my tears came from my pride in Jack's performance, the overall circumstance of how we celebrated, or not being able to breathe behind the mask I wore. I barely got the words out. In some respects, I'm glad I could hide behind a mask so others couldn't see my tear-stained face.

They say a parent will do anything to make their child happy. That declaration should come with caveats, and sometimes, parents should have their heads examined. But I would have never denied the thoughtful request from Jack to be his b'nei mitzvah partner and share this unforgettable day, no matter how we had to celebrate. No more sidelines and no more regrets.

The Real Housewife of the Hamptons

A FAVORITE CHILDHOOD memory is spending time with my family on Galveston, Corpus Christi, and Padre Island beaches in Texas. Even the warm waters of the Gulf of Mexico were invigorating. My mother always packed snacks, and we'd stop at the local fried chicken restaurant for lunch. She also made sure we had plenty of alcohol wipes to remove any tar residue off our bodies caused by the inevitable oil spills in the gulf.

Adam, who grew up in Southern California, also loved the beach. (The pristine Pacific Ocean wasn't as warm as the Gulf of Mexico but rarely had oil spills, though.) So naturally, the ocean became one of our favorite family pastimes.

We'd often take Jack on weekend day trips to the tony Hamptons, about ninety miles east of New York City. One evening, while driving back to the city, I started dreaming about how great it would be to own a home in the Hamptons.

"I wish we had a house out here, so we'd have a place to go every weekend," I told Adam. "Jack has so much fun at the beach, and I'm tired of the long drive."

"One day," Adam replied. "It's not out of the realm of possibility."

After several summers of dealing with that long drive and sitting in heavy traffic to enjoy a few hours on the beach, we got serious about finding our Hamptons getaway home. We hired a real estate broker to help us. The Hamptons includes two main towns: Southampton and East Hampton. Each has different areas called hamlets. And the further east you go, the more expensive it gets.

"What part of the Hamptons are you interested in living in?" Vanessa, our real estate agent, asked. "How far east do you want to go?"

"I want to be close to a beach. And not have to dip into Jack's college fund to pay for it," I said.

Vanessa and her partner, Jeremy, showed us several properties in the town of Southampton that were close to the beach and within our budget. We each had our area of importance in every house we viewed. Jack checked out the backyard and bedrooms to determine which would be his room. Adam's concern centered on the overall foundation of the house; he closely inspected the kitchen, where he'd be spending the most time. I ensured the house had a fireplace for cold winter nights and a pool for hot summer days. I also looked in each closet to guarantee we'd have enough space for our belongings, including all the junk in our Connecticut storage locker.

Jeremy and Vanessa found three properties for us to see one cold weekend in January. While the first one ticked most of the boxes with a big backyard, multiple bedrooms, a nice kitchen, and two fireplaces, it didn't have a pool. The spacious exterior allowed one to build a pool, but it backed up to a pig farm.

"I want a family pet, but I'd prefer a dog over a pig," I said.

The following two homes didn't work for us either. One had significant foundation structural issues. While beautifully designed, the other sat on a plain vanilla street that reminded me of the neighborhood in the movie *Poltergeist*. Every house looked the same, and for all I knew, ghosts lived in the basement.

We decided to expand our search further east to the hamlet of Hampton Bays.

"We have several more properties to show you that we think you'll love," Jeremy said.

We trekked to the Hamptons the following weekend to view more properties. The first home we toured, while beautiful and checked most of our boxes, didn't sit right with me for some reason.

"Is it me, or is this the nicest house on the block?" I asked Adam.

"It's not you. This house sticks out for all the wrong reasons," he said.

HGTV is my porn, and according to the *Property Brothers* and *House Hunters*, one of the most critical aspects to real estate is location, location, location, especially when it comes time to resell. The house was surrounded by a hodgepodge of homes that looked like they were thrown together to make a neighborhood. We decided to keep looking.

"The next two homes are on a beautiful tree-lined street. I believe you'll see all the houses look like they belong together," Jeremy said.

As we turned onto the street, we were immediately greeted by spacious homes with large yards and mature trees I assumed would look picturesque during the spring and summer. The first home sat on a flag lot, and as we drove down the long driveway, we were met with a contemporary home spanning just shy of an acre of land. The open living area with a fireplace was large and spacious, but no separate dining area existed.

"Where do you eat your meals? All I see is a small island in the kitchen," I said.

"I guess the owners don't entertain much," Adam speculated. "Besides, the kitchen is too small for my taste."

The next house was built in the 1980s and hadn't been updated since Reagan's inauguration. The backyard boasted a swimming pool and tennis court, but Adam wasn't convinced.

"This house falls under the 'bring your own architect' category. While I'd love to have a tennis court, I'm not ready to redo the entire foundation to repair that huge crack running down the middle of the court," he said.

And the rest of the house needed significant repairs as well.

"I think we'll keep looking," I told Jeremy.

"Good," he said. "If you told me you were interested, I would have talked you out of it. You'll spend more on repairs and updates than on the house."

Jeremy and Vanessa had one more house to show us in a beautiful tucked-away neighborhood.

The ranch-style home sat on one acre of land and had a pool, a koi pond, a fireplace, and a finished basement with a dry sauna that I initially thought was a panic room. I'd never seen a dry sauna in a house. It was within walking distance of the bay beaches and only a fifteen-minute drive to the Atlantic Ocean.

While the house checked many boxes, the kitchen needed major TLC. The cramped space had a small peninsula counter with outdated appliances, and a wall separated the kitchen from the main living space.

"Do you think we can take down this wall to open up the space for a larger kitchen?" I asked Adam.

"As long as the wall isn't holding up the house, I'm sure we can," he said.

Fortunately, the wall could come down and Adam could build his dream kitchen.

After we returned to the city following an exhaustive day of touring homes, the three of us sat down to have a family meeting.

"Are we doing this?" I asked.

"I love the last house," Jack said.

"Let's go for it," Adam said.

This was the first house Adam and I ever owned. I'd never possessed anything of this magnitude. While we'd continue living full-time in the city, I couldn't wait to spend our weekends and holidays in our new home. I pictured Jack growing up in the neighborhood, riding his bike with friends. But after a few years, I soon learned that even paradise gets boring.

. . .

We spent the summer of 2019 decorating, entertaining friends and family, and enjoying our new home. During the fall, we hired a contractor to renovate and update multiple rooms and areas, including knocking down the wall to build the kitchen.

"Whatever you want to do in this room is fine," I told Adam. "Clearly, you'll spend more time here than me."

Construction began on December 1, 2019. On March 12, 2020, our new kitchen appliances were plugged in, and we were in business. And not a minute too soon since everything in the world came to a screeching halt the same week when the country went on lockdown because of the COVID-19 pandemic. Adam's work went remote, as did Jack's school.

"I'm so happy we have our house to ride out this Covid night-mare," I said to Adam.

"Me too," he said.

While some construction projects like painting and cabinetry continued around us, we were fortunate to have the space to live and the opportunity to breathe fresh air outside.

The end of the 2020 school year arrived, and the world slowly began emerging from the pandemic nightmare, but nothing felt normal. Like so many of Jack's peers, he barely made it through his Zoom sixth-grade classes, and unfortunately, his grades suffered. Thankfully, in sixth grade, they didn't count for much.

We spent the summer going to the beach, hanging out by the pool, and enjoying the Hamptons. But as we approached the new school year, I began thinking about how Jack would survive another year of lockdowns and remote learning.

"What if school is fully remote again? Jack will not survive another year on Zoom, and I'll pull my hair out if he's at home all day," I said to Adam.

"Are there any schools out here he can attend that won't be fully remote? Maybe we'll move to our house full-time," he said.

"Yes, but what about your job? Won't you have to return to the office?"

"Eventually. But it won't be that bad going back and forth from the city."

After speaking to several moms in the neighborhood and at the beach, I discovered that schools on the east end of Long Island were not going remote. Instead, kids would be placed in "pods" by their grades. There were so many questions about returning to normalcy after the COVID shutdown. If it had only been "two weeks to stop the spread" as it was sold to Americans, our decisions would have been made for us. We would have returned to New York City, and our Hamptons home would be the weekend retreat we bought it for.

"If we move Jack to a school out here, we can keep an apartment in the city for when I need to be there for work. And you can be with your friends when I'm not there," Adam said.

While Adam tried to make our new normal sound appealing, I knew life post-COVID would not be the same, especially for me.

One morning, Adam, Jack, and I sat at our beautiful kitchen island for a family meeting to discuss options for the upcoming school year. Adam and I wanted Jack to be part of the decision, mainly because it impacted him the most.

"Jack, for seventh grade, would you rather continue at the Dwight School or go to a middle school closer to our home?" I asked.

"I want to go to school out here and not return to the city," he said. "I'll miss my friends, but I love our house and all the space."

I couldn't argue with him about space. Our new house had plenty of it, and we wasted no time filling each closet and storeroom to the rafters. Also, watching Jack be a kid and ride his bicycle around the neighborhood and hike the trails with other boys brought great joy to Adam and me.

While moving full-time to the Hamptons may sound glamorous, especially seeing the homes and lives of the *Real Housewives of New York City*, it was a big sacrifice, mainly for Adam and me. Once again, I had to start over, but this time in a mask. To make things more challenging, I wasn't allowed to go into Jack's school for over a year, and even then, I wore a face covering.

My good friends in the city were shocked and saddened to hear we were leaving New York City for the beach.

Many asked, "How can you leave the city? Won't you be bored?"

"Probably," I said. "But seeing how Jack has flourished in his new surroundings, I quickly realized sacrificing a tiny part of my happiness for his stability is a no-brainer."

Being an older mom helped me reach this realization faster than if I still lived my life thinking it was all about me. Or perhaps I was also ready for a change.

. . .

My heart ached when I dropped Jack off at his new middle school.

"Good luck, and you've got this," I said, not knowing what else to say. Of course, I wanted to say, "Don't be scared." But that statement was more about me than Jack.

I was confident my fear overshadowed his. My nerves rattled at the thought of Jack walking into a brand-new school in a mask, not knowing one person and me not knowing one parent or teacher. But kids are resilient and don't worry about things like adults.

"Mom, I'll be fine," he assured me. I couldn't help remembering his words on the first day of preschool: *Say goodbye, Mommy, I'm ready to play.*

Why wasn't Jack freaking out as much as I was?

Jack thrived in his new school and surroundings. We eventually got into a regular routine where Adam left Sunday night for the city and returned Wednesday night to work from home the rest of the week. I continued to be a work in progress. Driving every day became one of my most significant adjustments. I had gotten used to taking public transportation or walking everywhere, and now I had to remember to fill up the car with gas. I also missed my friends and the comforts of the place I'd called home for over twenty years. Life felt overwhelming and isolating, but the silver lining was a beautiful home and tons of space to roam.

Spending time alone and with my thoughts, I reignited a passion I never thought I'd follow: writing. Who knows whether I'd have revisited this desire if not for purchasing our Hamptons house. I've never been a fan of change. The unknown frightens me. But I've always lived my life with the understanding that things happen for a reason. I never dreamed we'd get to purchase a beach house in the Hamptons, much less decide to live in it full-time.

Living in New York City for over two decades, I never thought I'd live elsewhere. I also never believed I'd write and publish a book, proving dreams can emerge from boredom and solitude. And this is why my mother always taught me to *never* say never. Who knew a house at the beach would change the trajectory of my life?

Little Kid, Little Problems – Big Kid, Big Problems

The $6 Pee

ONE THING I HATED about having a nanny essentially raise Jack while I worked full-time was that she got to be present for significant milestones like crawling, saying new words, or holding a fork. Jack moved on from his crib when he was almost two years old. He didn't use words to tell us; rather, he showed us using action. Of course, Jack waited until Adam and I'd left for work, meaning our nanny, Desirée, experienced another one of Jack's milestones without us. However, I'm glad I wasn't home to see how he moved on.

"Judy, I don't know how to tell you this," Desirée said when she called me at work.

"Is everything okay? Is anyone hurt?"

"I put Jack in his crib for his morning nap and went into the other room. I heard a loud thump, and then Jack started crying. He was sitting on the floor when I ran into his room."

"Uh-oh," I said. "Is Jack okay?"

"Yes, he's fine. He startled himself, but not as much as he scared me."

"I guess it's time to transition to the toddler bed," I said with a laugh.

I was sad, knowing I missed another critical moment in Jack's life. But then again, did I want to see him hurling out of his crib?

While I missed out on many of Jack's firsts, I didn't mind Desirée's help with other things, especially potty training. Every parenting book warns that boys are notoriously difficult to potty train, and Jack didn't disappoint. The biggest waste of money and time were those little pee-pee teepees. I could have used a coffee filter and netted the same result.

"Jack, honey, let's try and use the potty tonight," I'd sweetly tell him before bedtime.

My mother kept saying he'd be ready when he was ready. But I was ready for him to be ready now. I was so over diapers!

Enter Desirée.

"I'll work with him. It just takes time and patience," she said one morning as I walked out the door for work.

Time and patience. Two things I didn't have.

. . .

While sitting at my desk one afternoon, Desirée called.

"Judy, it's been a bad day for Jack and me with potty training. He is so upset, and I think I've worn him out; I feel terrible," she said.

I could hear the anguish in her voice.

"Oh my gosh, don't get upset. I'm on my way home now, but in the meantime, take off Jack's diaper and put his underwear on him. Put him down for his nap. He'll probably have an accident, but that's okay. I'll clean it up when I get home," I said.

Before I left the office, I called Adam to tell him about my plan.

"On the way home from work, please stop at Home Depot and buy a tarp to cover all our rugs," I told him. "It's operation potty train this weekend, and by Monday, Jack better be fully trained, or I may be institutionalized."

I'd read on a parenting website that sometimes you need to rip off the diaper and let them have an accident, so I decided to try that. I was afraid if I didn't do something drastic, Jack would have a bowel obstructtion since, at this point, he hadn't used the bathroom for almost two days.

On the way home, I stopped at the corner bodega and picked up a flower bouquet to give to Desirée. She deserved more than flowers that day, but I didn't have time to stop at Tiffany's to buy her a piece of jewelry. I knew she felt that she'd let me down. But she did me a favor by getting the hard work out of the way.

When Adam got home, we covered all the rugs and let Jack run around the house bare-bottomed. He had precisely one accident. By Sunday night, he was fully potty-trained at three years and two months old. The operation was a huge success, but I'm confident it wouldn't have worked without Desirée's help.

. . .

Several weeks later, while driving home from a shopping mall in New Jersey, Jack announced he needed to use the bathroom. Of course, before leaving the mall, I'd asked if he needed to use the restroom, and he had said no.

"Can you please hold it until we can find a place to stop?" I begged him as I frantically searched for a truck stop off the interstate.

"No, Mommy. I can't hold it," he cried.

"Adam, pull off the highway and let him pee on the side of the road," I said.

I assumed his being a little boy would make it much easier for him to do this, but I prayed it wouldn't become a habit.

"Mommy, no, I don't want to go outside," Jack screamed.

"But honey, if you can't hold it, you'll have an accident. I'll make sure no one sees you," I said.

He refused. So, we drove on. Since we were close to Newark Airport, Adam decided to get off the highway and go to the Marriott Hotel on the airport property.

"Please hurry," I said to him.

"I have to get a parking ticket because you can't park for free at an airport," he replied.

Adam pulled the ticket from the machine and raced to the front of the hotel. I grabbed the diaper bag I kept with me that contained everything but diapers, and Jack and I ran inside to the bathroom.

"I didn't make it," Jack said.

I could tell he was devastated, so I tried to comfort him.

"It's okay, honey," I assured him. "Accidents happen."

While I didn't have diapers in the diaper bag, I did have a change of clothes. I changed Jack's underwear and pants and stuffed the wet clothes into the bag. I'd have to remember to take them out as soon as we got home.

Adam joined us as we walked out of the restroom.

"He almost made it. I got a little too confident thinking I'd be able to ditch the diapers," I said.

"It's okay, Jack," Adam said, also assuring him.

We left the hotel lobby and returned to the car to drive home. Adam handed the parking ticket to the gate attendant.

"That will be six dollars," the attendant said.

"The six-dollar pee!" Adam said.

Nothing in life is free.

SpongeBob & The Berenstain Bears Give Advice

I ALWAYS WONDERED WHERE my parents got the words of wisdom they so often used on my sister, Celia, and me. You'll remember them as I'm sure some of these pearls were used on you too: "Don't cry over spilled milk" and "Money doesn't grow on trees" and "Turn out the lights; I don't own shares in the electric company."

While I took their advice with a grain of salt (I'm sure I got that line from my parents too), I remember wondering how they were so wise. My parents always seemed to have a response ready whenever I asked or tried to do something I knew they wouldn't approve of, or that I would never get away with, even if I were only thinking about it.

Then I had my own child, and suddenly I understood. My parents didn't make these sayings up. They probably got them from their parents or heard them from somewhere else and just tried to pass them off as their own. Brilliant!

But what does one do if their young son starts offering his words of wisdom before one gets a chance to pass pearls of wisdom along to him? And what happens if said child's advice comes from a cartoon character named SpongeBob SquarePants?

When Jack was about four and first became interested in TV cartoon characters, I was thrilled that he loved Cookie Monster,

Curious George, and the Cat in the Hat. I used to joke that at least he wasn't watching Barney the purple dinosaur or SpongeBob Square-Pants. I was a bit premature in that observation.

One afternoon, Jack and I were walking home from school. We discussed what he was learning and working on.

"Jack, I'm very impressed with your schoolwork and how well you're doing," I told him.

"Mommy, you can't rush perfection," he matter-of-factly replied.

What?!

"Where did you hear that phrase?" I questioned him.

"SpongeBob said it," he said proudly.

I almost fainted.

My young child is learning life advice from a sponge!

Adam and I tried watching as many SpongeBob episodes with Jack as possible, so we knew what was filling his brain. We also bought several DVDs of the program so Jack could watch them on the car's rear entertainment system. Truth: once I got past SpongeBob's annoying laugh and the opening theme song, I found it entertaining. Not educational, but at least not offensive.

After watching the show on repeat, I picked up pearls of wisdom that I borrowed from the little yellow sponge and passed along to Jack, because a mother needs all the help she can get:

1. Never give up on anything.
2. Friendships are the most critical relationships in your life.
3. Hard work and perseverance lead to good things.
4. Be a good neighbor.
5. Enjoy life to the fullest.

It is not lost on me that these are similar to the life lessons passed on by my parents, and I'm confident that Jack will one day pass these along to his children. Of course, with the good comes the bad, as one of his other favorite quotes from Mr. Krabs became "A five-letter word for happiness is M-O-N-E-Y."

. . .

One morning, as I stood in the bathroom getting ready for the day, Jack, who was six at the time, came to me with the most serious look.

"Mommy, please turn off the blow dryer. I have a question," he said.

Even though half my head was still wet, I complied because this moment felt important.

"What is it, honey? Are you okay?"

With a scrunched brow, he thoughtfully asked, "Mommy, does showing your middle finger to someone mean you don't like the president?"

You can imagine how hard it was to keep a straight face, but I did. I tried to summon up all the parenting knowledge I'd been stockpiling through the years from reading article after article on how to deal with situations precisely like this one. Like an eraser to a chalkboard, my mind went blank.

"Honey, why do you think this?" I asked him, not knowing if I wanted the answer.

"I heard it at camp," he said.

Of course, summer camp: the place to make friends, have fun, and learn a lifetime of bad habits from other kids.

This was not the first time I'd been confronted with the word associated with the middle finger. When Jack was about five, I stood in the stall as he used the bathroom at Palm Beach Airport. When we finished, he noticed the f-word scratched into the wall.

In his loudest outside voice, he asked, "What does f**k mean?"

I tried to ignore him (and the laughter I heard outside) and said, "It's a bad word we don't use, and if you do, I'll wash your mouth out with every type of soap you can find in the soap aisle at Target."

I knew this practice and the taste of Irish Spring all too well from my youth, so naturally, I'd use the same threat with Jack. I'm not innocent regarding foul language; some may even say I have a sailor's mouth. I always thought God's last name was dammit because my father threw the phrase around effortlessly. Adam isn't innocent either, and we tried hard to refrain from using foul language around Jack in his formative years, but "stuff" happens, and old habits are hard to break.

While we were in the car one afternoon, Adam got a little salty when a reckless driver cut him off.

"Hey, f**k you!" Adam yelled.

The driver shot Adam the bird as he passed our car.

"Screw you, a**hole!" Adam yelled back.

"Adam, watch the language," I warned. "Little ears hear everything."

I was far from perfect, though. As I walked into Jack's bedroom one evening, barefoot, I smashed my foot on the rocking chair and broke my toe.

"G-d dammit!" I yelled. "Mother-f**king chair!"

Jack sat still on the floor and just looked at me. At least Adam wasn't home to hear me swear in front of Jack.

. . .

As parents, no matter our age, we always look for resources to help teach our children right from wrong and the importance of things like getting along with our friends, sharing, saying please and thank you, telling the truth, having manners, and not using potty-mouth language.

Early on, I found that some of the best books to help me teach Jack these crucial lessons were not on the shelves of Barnes & Noble's parenting section. Instead, I turned to the Berenstain Bears. Yes, the family of Mama, Papa, Brother Bear, and Sister Bear, who live in a tree house down a sunny dirt road deep in Bear Country, became my go-to teachers. Some of our favorite titles included: *The Truth*, *Forget Their Manners*, *The Green-Eyed Monster*, *Too Much Junk Food*, *Get the Gimmies*, and *The In-Crowd*. While each book was relatable to children, as a bonus (at least for me), they helped parents to reinforce lessons.

After the question of the middle finger and insulting the president came up, I tried to do my best Berenstain Bear imitation.

"Jack, sometimes adults and children say foul words and use inappropriate gestures," I said.

Not missing a beat, Jack asked, "Does giving the middle finger have anything to do with that word from the bathroom at Palm Beach Airport?"

I can't win.

"Yes, but using that gesture is unkind and has nothing to do with liking or disliking the president, no matter your politics," I said.

I looked at my half-dried head of hair in the mirror and decided it was a lost cause, so I put it up in a ponytail. As we went out the door, I noticed Jack still looked puzzled.

"Do you have more questions?" I prayed he didn't. I wasn't prepared to answer where babies come from that morning.

"No. But I guess Mama and Papa Bear don't have to worry about talking to Brother and Sister about the middle finger."

"Why is that?" I asked.

"Because they only have four fingers," he said.

Dear Jack, Today You Are Ten

WHEN JACK TURNED TEN, it hit me like a ton of bricks. Mainly because that meant I had turned fifty-three a few months earlier. But him being ten felt so far from being a baby and too close to him growing up. I knew I had to strap in for the next ten years, especially as he hit the dreaded teenage phase.

Jack loved turning ten. He walked around the house holding up two hands in celebration. It's easy to forget the simple things that make your child happy. While I didn't write him a letter for each birthday, turning ten felt so monumental I thought I'd put my emotions and thoughts into words.

Dear Jack,

And then you were ten. Wow, today you, my baby boy, turn ten years old. If I've heard it once, I've heard it a million times: enjoy the early years because they pass in the blink of an eye. I now understand.

Ten years. A whole decade. A half generation. Even though I'm the parent and teacher of all things right and wrong for you, these past ten years, I've been just as much your student as you are mine.

Over the past ten years, I have learned so much more about myself through your eyes, and something tells me you have so much more to teach me in the years to come. But I find it miraculous that as you've aged, somehow, I haven't (at least in my mind). I hope that continues.

While it's impossible to sum up all the things you've taught me over the past ten years, here's a condensed list of ten of my favorites:

1. *French fries are a food group.*
2. *The New York City subway system is a true adventure.*
3. *Laughing until you pee your pants is a good thing.*
4. *SpongeBob SquarePants teaches life lessons despite his annoying laugh.*
5. *Little eyes and ears see and hear everything—and little mouths repeat most things too.*
6. *Potty humor and fart jokes are hilarious.*
7. *You got your father's eyes and your mother's mouth (and not just my smile).*
8. *I still don't like math, especially geometry.*
9. *Board games and Lego building are still fun all these years later.*
10. *Unconditionally loving someone is a powerful and intense feeling.*

I'm so excited to see what the future holds for you. You're full of life with a never-ending curiosity and an insatiable thirst for knowledge, especially technology. These traits will lead you to great things in life and, hopefully, the creation of the next million-dollar app.

My birthday wishes for you today, and for many years to come, are to believe you can do great things in your life and never give up on yourself, no matter what. You have so many unique gifts, and your infectious smile and incredible personality bring joy to many people.

Ten years ago (after twenty long hours of labor), you burst into my world, and I wouldn't change you, or these past ten years, for anything. I thank God every day you came into my life, and I'm so blessed and proud to be your mom.

I'll always love you more!

. . .

Several years have passed since I wrote this letter, but so much of what I said still holds, especially the part about Jack being my teacher in life. Being forty-three when Jack came into my world, I worried about relating to him and being so much older. Here's the thing about kids: they don't care how old you are. They also don't care what you look like in a bathing suit.

As parents, we think we'll have a certain kind of kid, like one who doesn't challenge us and listens, obeys, and doesn't talk back. But that kid doesn't exist. And thank goodness for that! Every child is unique, and all we can do is guide them to make good choices, respect others, and not do something that lands them in jail.

Advice to My High Schooler

I SAT IN THE AUDIENCE THE evening of Jack's middle school graduation and cried, not out of sadness but pride. I realized Jack was only moving up to high school, and this event wasn't his college graduation, but for some reason, it felt so much more to me than a simple ceremony.

At this point, I'd sat through a pre-K and kindergarten graduation, but these formalities were mainly staged for parents to gather for coffee and cake and ensure you cleaned out your child's cubby at the end of the school year.

I had much to tell Jack on the ceremony day, but I knew I'd start crying. He hates it when I cry. Instead, I wrote him a letter. The letter's intent wasn't to make Jack sad. I wanted to pass on any wisdom I could remember from when I was his age. The moving up ceremony to high school experience hit me hard. Emotions flooded my thoughts, knowing this event marked the beginning of many significant milestones for Jack.

It reminded me how fortunate I was to watch him grow from a baby to now. I didn't often speak of my prior pregnancy losses before Jack was born, especially to him. There was nothing to say. I'd given up hope of ever having a child, so having Jack at forty-three made me think of him as my little miracle and most significant accomplishment. I now prayed we'd both survive high school and beyond.

Dear Jack,

Today, you graduated eighth grade, middle school. I realize it may not have the same status as graduating from high school or college, as so many of my friends' children are celebrating this year; clearly, my friends are much older than me, something you've never noticed or mentioned before. And I'll always love you for believing me when I tell you I'm twenty-nine.

However, today is still a huge milestone you should be proud of reaching. As your mom and biggest cheerleader, I'm incredibly proud of you and completely overwhelmed.

Things sure have changed since I was a schoolgirl. For starters, I didn't have a moving up ceremony to high school. The only thing we did on the last day was run through the halls singing "School's Out," Alice Cooper's end-of-school anthem that still makes me smile and always reminds me of summer. But the world is a different place today, a sentiment shared by parents everywhere as they pass the torch from generation to generation.

As I watched you walk across the stage this evening, shaking hands with your teachers and the faculty, I felt moments of pure excitement and sheer terror. My excitement was for all the opportunities, memories, and experiences you will have as you enter high school. My terror lay on my ability to shield you and help guide you through the turbulence you have no idea is coming your way. And you better strap in because it will be a bumpy ride, or maybe that's just for me. I've been thinking a lot about how I can help you without it seeming like I'm helping you. I get it; moms aren't that cool anymore and can be annoying. Believe it or not, I was your age once, albeit a "few" years back. So, I thought I'd give you my best "cool mom" high school advice, and you can take it or leave it. But if I were you, I'd take it since I've been in your shoes before.

Friendships: *Unlike your family and relatives, you can pick your friends. Choose wisely and understand you don't have to be friends with everyone, and not everyone will be your bestie.*

Crushes & Heartbreak: *This will be a roller-coaster ride. Fortunately for you, I have years of experience in both areas, so talk to me. And rest assured, the first person who breaks your heart will have to deal with me. Good luck to them!*

Puberty: *I'd like to leave this topic to your dad, but I'm a realist. You will have many questions as your body goes through different changes. It's okay; I'm your mom, the woman who gave birth to you. Trust me, I've seen worse. You're going to smell, so please bathe regularly and use deodorant.*

School & Homework: *The shit just got real! Let me give you some advice: like you play video games, treat your homework assignments and classes like a challenge you can achieve, conquer, and slay. Homework will be complicated; you'll be bored, but you have no choice. Try your best, and don't be afraid to ask for help. But please don't ask me to help you with math. That's your dad's area.*

Technology & Social Media: *Yes, I know you're already more intelligent than I am in all things computers, bits, and bytes, but hear this warning: if you put it out there in the digital universe, it doesn't disappear with a stroke of the delete button. Friendships and reputations can be damaged beyond repair by what you put out in cyberspace. Yes, the Golden Rule still applies in the digital world. Yes, I did stupid things when I was your age. Fortunately, you'll never find it on the internet.*

Be a kid, but grow up! *Believe it or not, you're still only fourteen years old. And while we think kids are growing up faster and faster these days, so did* *our parents and their parents before them. It's okay to stop and enjoy the moment, wreak havoc, and cause a little trouble, just not too much trouble.*

A parent's primary goal is to help shape and raise independent, caring, respectful, loving children, not jerks. And you, my middle school graduate, tick all the boxes. When I dropped you off at preschool, and you stated, "Say goodbye, Mommy, I'm ready to play," I knew you were a force. As you embark on the road to high school in the fall, no matter the challenges you face, I'll always be in your corner cheering you on to success. You're going to have good and bad days ahead— as will I, so go easy on me—but I have so much faith and confidence in you and can't wait to watch you shine.

I love you to the moon and back and with all my heart, and I'm so proud to be your mom!

Heaven knows the world is different than it was all those years ago when I entered high school. In some ways, my age and experiences are a bonus as I've seen it all. I want to make sure Jack benefits from my successes and failures and uses them to navigate the rough waters of the next phase of his life. I pray the seas won't be as choppy, but I'll be there to throw him a life jacket if he ever feels like he's drowning.

Digital Heroin

I'M CONVINCED NO ONE would have kids if parents remembered how horrible they were during their teenage years. Parenting teenagers has always been challenging, or so my mother reminds me. As a child of the seventies and eighties, my exposure to temptations was plentiful, mainly drugs. While there were times when my adventurous spirit and curiosity got the best of me, thankfully my personality was such that I never went any further than that initial interest. Well, most of the time.

If you're a member of Generation X, you remember the infamous Public Service Announcement (PSA) that ran on TV called "This Is Your Brain on Drugs." In it, a man, presumably someone's dad, is holding an egg and a frying pan, with the egg representing the brain. He proceeds to crack the egg into the frying pan and, once it's all scrambled, says, "This is your brain on drugs. Any questions?"

The PSA presented powerful messaging for its time. Strangely, it's even more relevant today, not just as it relates to the actual drug epidemic sweeping our nation but to children's overuse of technology devices. If somebody made a PSA for today's generation, the VR headset or Xbox would replace your brain, and a screenshot of an angry Creeper attacking a Mine-craft world or a guy stealing a car in *Grand Theft Auto* would represent the brain on too much technology.

When Jack was seven years old, he got off the camp bus and said, "Mom, everyone has an iPhone, iTouch, or iPad. Why can't I have one of these too?"

Instead of answering directly, I did what any self-respecting parent of a seven-year-old begging for these items while desperately trying to teach their child that there was more to life than handheld technology devices would do: I changed the subject.

"How was camp today? Did you have fun swimming and playing games?" I asked.

He ignored me, but my deflection worked as he dropped the subject.

The following day, I stood at the camp bus stop with Emily, a mom friend from my apartment building whose children attended camp with Jack.

"Did you see all the kids get off the bus yesterday with iPads and cell phones?" she asked.

"Yes, and honestly, I'm not surprised. I don't care that the kids have them. I'm upset that they're using them in front of my kid because he now wants his own devices," I said.

Talk about peer pressure. I can only imagine the con-versation in the home of one of these children if they happened to leave the iPad or cell phone on the bus or it got stolen. Would the parent be upset with the child or themselves?

It's not that I was against Jack or any other child using technology at a young age—far from it. Nor am I one to pass judgment on how others parent their children; heaven knows I'm not perfect. I just believed there was a time and place for said devices, and summer camp was not one of them. The parent camp handbook agreed with me too, but I guess some parents skipped that page.

There were days when I succumbed to the technology temptation and gave in to Jack just so I could have a conversation with Adam or get something done. Still, I didn't want Jack carrying a cell phone at seven years old.

Of course, maybe my initial hesitancy stemmed from watching how Jack treated our devices when he was five.

"Why won't the iMac boot up? And what's that rattling noise?" I asked Adam one day when trying to log on to our computer.

Turns out, Jack had used the CD-ROM opening on the side of the computer as a slot machine and stuffed coins inside. The Apple Genius Bar man informed us we weren't the first parents to bring their desktops in for repair with this issue. He slipped a magnetic strip inside the slot and out came $1.25.

Then, there was a time when Adam, Jack, and I ate dinner at a fish shack in New York City. Jack became restless and asked Adam for his iPhone to play a game.

"Be super careful and keep it on the table so it won't drop on the floor," Adam said.

Famous last words. A few minutes after Jack took the phone, he dropped it and it fell under the table.

"I'll get it," I told Adam as I crawled under the filthy table to retrieve the phone.

I could feel Adam's anger.

"Don't even tell me the phone doesn't work anymore," Adam said.

I examined the phone, and miraculously, there wasn't a scratch on it.

"Nope," I said. "We dodged a bullet this time."

When we got in the car to go home from the restaurant, Adam tried plugging his phone into the charger, but the cable kept slipping out as if it wouldn't connect. Worse, the phone wouldn't turn on.

"That's strange," Adam said. "I'll have to take it to the Apple Genius Bar and let them see what's happening."

Fortunately, we lived down the block from an Apple Store, a good thing since we spent many hours at the Genius Bar.

Adam came home from the Apple Store shaking his head.

"Is your phone working now?" I asked.

"Yes, because I have a new phone," he replied.

"What, why?" I asked.

"The phone appears okay on the outside," he said. "But when the guy at the Genius Bar shined a flashlight inside the phone, he found something stuck. He took a pair of tweezers to grab it and pulled out a sliver of a french fry."

I stared at Adam in disbelief.

"He said the salt from the french fry shorted out the internal wiring and shut down the phone."

"Unlike coins in the slot opening of an iMac, I'm assuming a french fry in an iPhone was a first for the Genius Bar?" I asked.

"Yes," Adam said.

"At least we gave them a new problem-solving idea and a good story for future customers."

As parents, we should decide when and how our kids use technology. I mean, even top tech executives from Google, YouTube, and Facebook have admitted to not letting their children have devices or sit in front of screens for hours using the inventions they've created. Now they tell us.

Today's adolescents are no different from any other generation when screaming "Mom, that's not fair!" or declaring "You just don't understand because life was so different when you were my age." Plus, spending more time in the virtual world than in the real world makes it even more difficult for parents to find common ground and connect with their kids. If we don't get a firm grip on technology usage while our kids are in their formative years, the struggles will continue as they age. If only I understood this theory when Jack was younger.

. . .

When Jack entered middle school, I tried to have a conversation with him one afternoon.

"How can I talk to you when you have a virtual reality set strapped to your head or your face is glued to a video game screen?"

He rolled his eyes and replied, "Hold on and let me finish. You know I can't stop the game once I start it." And then he added, "Oh, Mom, you know how much I love technology."

And sometimes, these conversations didn't even happen in person. One afternoon, while sitting at my computer writing, my phone went wild with text alerts from Jack. At first, I thought it was a real emergency since multiple messages came in at once.

Mom, quick, you have to order the new strap for my VR set because they only have one left in stock.

I didn't reply.

Two seconds later, another text came through.

Hello, Mom! Are you there?

I still didn't reply.

Two seconds after that, another text.

Why are you ignoring me? I must talk to you!

Now it was my turn to roll my eyes.

I laughed at how much I thought my parents didn't "get me" and how I acted far superior to their guidance. Here's the truth: having children in your twenties and thirties means your age is closer to your teenager's age, but your life experience is not as complete. Having children in your forties or later, however, means you've lived an entire lifetime, sometimes making it harder to relate to these young creatures.

Parents using technology today as a crutch to keep their kids entertained is equivalent to my friends who used the VCR as a babysitter. The only difference is that VCRs are obsolete, and smartphones and iPads are here to stay.

We live in a technologically advanced society, and there's no hiding from it. But weaning our kids off devices, at least according to many professionals, is like weaning someone off drugs or alcohol or chocolate: you can't do it overnight.

I'm guilty of using too much technology, especially with my head in my iPhone 24/7, playing Candy Crush, or watching videos on Instagram. I'm also known to text Adam or Jack inside the house to ask them a question. Does that mean I'm teaching by example? I can only hope Jack's never-ending curiosity and insatiable thirst for knowledge, especially in technology, will lead to the creation of a multibillion dollar company primed for an IPO. But first, he needs to put down his phone and be part of society in the real world, not a virtual one.

Music to My Ears

I'M CONSIDERED A BABY BOOMER, having been born in 1964, the last year of the baby boom wave (1946–1964). But I've always associated more with Generation X (1965–1980) because I never felt like a baby boomer. In fact, even though I spent barely five years growing up in the sixties, I don't remember much about the decade. As the saying goes, "If you remember the sixties, you really weren't there." While technically I was born, I wasn't part of its generation.

My generation grew up in the seventies and eighties. When you talk to a lot of people (mainly baby boomers and older) about their most significant memories from the seventies and eighties, many automatically recall events and people such as the Vietnam War, Richard Nixon, Watergate, Jimmy Carter, the Iran hostage crisis, inflation, gas lines, groovy fashion, shoulder pads, big hair, boycotting the Olympics, Ronald Reagan, and so much more.

When you ask anyone from Generation X about this era, we may recall those events, trends, and people, but most (specifically me) love talking about music. We bought LPs, 45s, 8-tracks, and cassettes, and get this—when we bought new music in any form, we invited friends over to our homes or went to their house and listened to it together.

As an older mom, one area that has leveled the playing field for Jack and me is music. While I'll never be able to compete for my son's attention with video games and technology, I have the upper hand in music. Music has been a big part of my life ever since my father used to blast his hi-fi stereo (that he built) playing all the great artists from Frank Sinatra to Neil Diamond to the Beatles. There was always music on in our house. Like my teenage son, my father and I were generations apart on most things. Still, we enjoyed a shared love for music, although he didn't always prefer my musical tastes.

I remember my first concert: KC and The Sunshine Band at the Houston Livestock Show & Rodeo in 1977. Yes, at twelve years old, I was shaking my booty and doing the hustle among the horses and livestock. It was awesome.

That show began my love of concerts, specifically rock concerts, and the louder, the better. You always knew a concert was good when you left the arena with ringing ears or a hoarse voice. And because I took great pride in knowing the words to every song on the radio, I loved to sing (scream) along as if I were part of the band. My mother often said that if I had known my schoolwork as well as the words to every single song, I would have been valedictorian of my class.

My generation didn't have iPods and Apple Music; we listened to the radio and Casey Kasem's American Top 40 weekly to know which 45s (small vinyl discs) to buy. Record stores provided printed copies of the Top 40 playlists each week. A former boyfriend, Randy, collected them; knowing him, he probably still has every single one.

My love of music steered me toward a radio and record promotion career. I programmed music for rock, contemporary, and high-energy dance radio stations. My friends and I attended hundreds of live concerts with all the greats: Elton John, Billy Joel, the Rolling Stones, Paul McCartney, Michael Jackson, Bruce Springsteen, and many more. I also promoted musical artists, including pop trio Wilson Phillips and the one-hit-wonder rapper Vanilla Ice. Even after leaving the music industry for different jobs, I never strayed far from my love of music and prayed I'd one day share this passion with my child.

. . .

When Jack was in eighth grade and I was driving him to school one day, he said, "I'm in charge of the music."

At first, I sighed and rolled my eyes because if I had to hear a crazy rap or hip-hop song again, I might drive the car off the road. So, imagine my delight when he switched the radio to the classic rock station. While listening to Van Halen's "Jump" and Def Leppard's "Photograph," my pride swelled as I shared a piece of my past with Jack.

"When did you start listening to this music?" I asked.

"It's what my friends and I like," he said.

This was music to my ears, pun intended.

We don't own a stereo system for our home, but we have several Bluetooth speakers. Jack and I enjoy blasting classic rock tunes from the speakers while hanging by the pool and sometimes, we play music while making dinner or baking cookies. Our impromptu rock 'n roll parties are some of my favorite moments.

I'm not surprised my son is fond of this era of music since, as an infant, in addition to the standards like "Rockabye Baby" and "Mary Had a Little Lamb," I filled his room with classic rock lullabies by the Beatles, Led Zeppelin, Fleetwood Mac, the Who, and more.

When he first started understanding song lyrics, one of his favorite tunes became "You Can't Always Get What You Want" by the Rolling Stones. This was his anthem, and a teachable moment. This song helped us teach him that just because you want something doesn't mean you get it, but if you try hard, you might get what you need. Who knew Mick and the boys would be a resource for such great parental advice?

At a sleepover in the fourth grade, Jack was asked by the parents of his friend what music he wanted to listen to. When he replied Supertramp, they were thrilled and shocked by his sophisticated musical preference.

"How does he know about Supertramp?" the dad later asked me.

"Because I love the band and play their music all the time," I said.

Jack also had a fondness for the Eagles' "Hotel California" and Jimmy Buffet's "Margaritaville." We often walked to his swim lesson each week singing both songs. I'd forgotten most of the words over the years and relearned them to sing along with Jack.

The invention of Spotify and satellite radio makes it even easier to share this musical experience with Jack in the car through playlists and radio stations like Classic Vinyl and Classic Rewind. It's a lot better than carrying a cassette or CD case in the car as I used to do at his age.

Of course, explaining to him how the needle on the record player read the music on the vinyl, or what the yellow plastic thingamajig was that went into the hole on a 45, or how you had to rewind and fast-forward the cassette tape, or even what a cassette tape deck looked like (forget trying to explain 8-tracks) makes me feel ancient. But I love our connection through these relics of yesteryear.

While I no longer have the more than four hundred record albums I once possessed, I do have boxes and boxes of CDs. When Adam and I first married, we combined our CD collections and housed them into a CD carousel changer that held hundreds of discs. Like me, Adam's collection included classic rock greats. We no longer own a CD player, but Jack can play the discs through our DVD player.

In addition to listening to classic rock music, Jack now plays the guitar and piano, and he has learned to play Pink Floyd's "Another

Brick in the Wall," Deep Purple's "Smoke on the Water," and Led Zeppelin's "Stairway to Heaven."

There's a great T-shirt that says, "I may be old, but I've seen all the cool bands." I won't lie; I feel like a cool mom driving down the street blaring AC/DC or Van Halen out of the speakers in a sing-along with Jack. Sadly, like me, this music is now considered classic and old. This leaves me scratching my head and asking, "When did that happen?"

Beware of the Hefty Trash Bag

DURING MY TEENAGE YEARS (and beyond), my mother said I had an acid tongue. She'd often say, "Judy, that sassy mouth will get you in trouble one day." I now understand what she meant.

Being a woman in her fifties with a teenager, I realize my own teenage days are years in my rearview mirror, but my gawd, did I give my mother this much attitude? I couldn't have acted this poorly as an adolescent. Or had I?

Of course, some memories never fade, like being sent straight to my room when my sister and I decided to purposefully spill our drinks at the table, or getting a stern look from my father that meant if I even thought of continuing down the path of destructive behavior I probably wouldn't sit down for a week, or having my mouth washed out with soap when I sassed back to my mother. Aw, the good old days. My oh my, how times have changed.

And there's no more significant change than when it comes to dealing with the teenage attitude. What is with the angst? What does this generation have to be angry about? Are they tired of getting everything they want? The "everyone's a winner" way of thinking is creating a generation of entitled brats.

Before the start of each school year, I loved school supply shopping with my mother. Something about buying new pens, pencils, notebooks, folders, and liquid paper made me so happy. Naturally, when the time came for school supply shopping with Jack, I imagined he'd be as excited as I had been in high school.

"We're going to buy new school supplies. I need your list," I said.

"Just pick up whatever you want. I don't care," he said.

His lack of enthusiasm crushed me. But he finally agreed to accompany me to Staples, and we went to stock up and prepare him for the new school year.

"You're going to need new folders for each class. Let's get eight folders to make sure you have enough," I said.

"I only need five folders for English, math, science, social studies, and electives. That's all I need," he said.

"What about Spanish and your two elective classes?" I asked.

"I only need one for electives; I don't need separate folders," he snapped.

"But you should have extra folders," I said.

And in the nastiest, most annoyed retort, he said, "Should I get a folder for lunch too?"

I stared at him in disbelief.

Excuse me for preparing you.

Even though smoke was forming in my head and getting ready to blow through my ears, I knew whatever I said to Jack would be heard by all the parents and their children standing in earshot. I should have left the store with no new supplies, but that meant I'd have to return to buy everything anyway. We left the store with eight folders.

Later that night, as I retold the folder story to my mother, she said, "I would have smacked him right there in the middle of Staples."

"And that's why your generation would be in jail with how you raised children," I replied.

I've often told my mother that by today's standards, she and my father would probably be in prison based on their disciplinary styles from way back when. Of course, I went to school when corporal punishment was acceptable and getting in trouble in class most certainly meant a trip to the principal's office and probable detention. Why did those days have to end?

Today, parents call in their lawyers, and the next morning, they're all on *Good Morning America* pleading their case. Don't get me wrong, some horrible kids are doing terrible things, and vice versa with some parents. But whatever happened to consequences and the fear of God from your mother and father?

. . .

As a teenager, I was no angel. I gave my parents a massive amount of attitude and expected them to do everything I asked. In other words, I was a brat. But I never did anything to make them call in lawyers, or at least I'd like to think not.

I was also a total slob. And no surprise, so is Jack.

"Do you not see the clothes hamper in the corner of your room?" I ask him every morning upon entering his bedroom and stepping over a pile of dirty clothes on the floor.

"Yes, Mom, I do," he says with a grunt.

"Is there a reason you leave your clothes and wet towels on the floor?" I ask.

"No," he responds.

While it would be easy to pick up the clothes, put them in the hamper, and hang the wet towels in the bathroom, I don't.

"You're going to make a great husband one day," I say with sarcasm.

I've shed my youth's messy, disorganized ways and am now a neat freak. Even though it kills me to be greeted by the mess of Jack's bedroom with piles of clothes sitting next to the hamper, candy wrappers, half-eaten food, and water bottles strewn about, I can't help but laugh and shake my head, knowing I was the same way.

My mother prohibited my father from entering my room un-announced for fear he'd kick me out of the house. She also made a deal with our housekeeper, Shirley, to stay away until I cleaned up my mess.

"Shirley is forbidden to clean your room until you take responsi-bility," she told me.

"That's not fair," I whined. "I promise I'll do better if you let Shirley clean it today."

Fortunately, Shirley and I were buddies, so she cleaned my room, even though I always had difficulty fulfilling my end of the bargain.

My bedroom should have been condemned and declared a disaster zone, especially on one Thanksgiving holiday weekend.

The night before Thanksgiving, I'd gone out with friends while my sister stayed home and helped my mother prepare our dinner. I was also a selfish teenager who couldn't be bothered to help when needed. Celia and my mother decided to prank me. They put the turkey carcass into a Hefty garbage bag and then placed the bag under the covers of my unmade bed, assuming I'd never see it. When I returned home and walked into the house, I noticed they were on the phone.

"Who are you talking to this late? I asked. "And why are y'all laughing?"

"We're talking to your uncle Joe, and he told us a funny joke," my mom said.

"Tell him hi for me. I'm going to bed," I said.

I walked into my bedroom, wading through the pile of clothes on the floor, and climbed into bed. I noticed the garbage bag.

Why is this garbage bag in my bed?

I stuck my hand inside the bag and started screaming.

My father ran down the hall to see about the commotion as my mother and sister ran upstairs, laughing so hard I thought one or both would wet their pants.

"We wanted to see if you'd even notice we put the turkey carcass in your bed since this is where everything goes to die."

My family had a sick sense of humor.

Sometimes, Jack throws my messy teenage days in my face when I nudge him about being a slob.

"How can you get mad at me for being messy when you never cleaned your room as a teenager?" he sarcastically asked.

He was correct, but fortunately, I grew out of my slob phase. I pray Jack grows out of these days too, sooner rather than later. Yes, I've threatened to keep the housekeeper out of Jack's room if he doesn't pick up his mess. But if I were him, I'd be careful if he finds a trash bag in the middle of his bed.

Learning to Drive

SOMETIMES I LOOK AT Jack and wonder where I went wrong. This question mainly centers on his constant badgering of wanting what he wants, when he wants it, and not stopping until he gets it. I swear, one day, he'll become a lawyer.

But then there are days when I think, *Oh my gosh, you're exactly like me!*

There's no better example of our similarities than Jack's desire to learn to drive. When he turned fifteen, he begged me to let him practice driving.

"Mom, when can I learn to drive?" he asked me daily.

"When you're tall enough to reach the pedals," I'd reply.

But I realized this was a temporary response since I knew he'd one day tower over my five-foot-three frame.

In truth, the idea of Jack operating a vehicle frightens me more than what he looks like driving. I remember my relentless pestering, trying to wear down my parents, wondering when I could start driving the car. I now understand their frustration. But things were different when I was his age, a statement made by every parent before handing over the keys.

"Just because you've mastered the getaway car in video games doesn't mean you're ready to start driving," I said.

"Mom, it's just video games, and it's not like I'll be reckless and start stealing cars," he said.

That response gave me so much comfort. What is it with today's generation thinking they can learn anything and master everything, like driving a car or performing surgery, by watching a YouTube video?

"You know I can get a learner's permit and start driving when I turn sixteen. I should start practicing now," he said.

"Not in New York State," I told him.

Fortunately, living in New York State, Jack isn't eligible to get a learner's permit until he turns sixteen and a full driver's license at age seventeen. And that's only after passing driver's education. I love New York!

The conversations about learning to drive eerily reminded me of when I was about to turn sixteen. My one-track mind exhausted my mom and dad, and like my parents with me, I was not ready for the discussion or the act. This fact centered on what happened the day I finally got my driver's license.

In August 1980, I joined the ranks of licensed drivers when I narrowly passed my driver's ed test. It was a miracle I passed. During the driving exam, I drove up onto the curb of a house while backing around the corner.

"I guess I'll be retaking the test," I said to the instructor.

"No, you're good; I've been with worse drivers than you," he said as he white-knuckled the dashboard.

Geez, they'll give anyone a license.

While the instructor may have decided I deserved my license, my parents had a different idea. When I asked to use his car, my father told me, "You'll only be allowed to drive it during the day with one of us in it."

I had big dreams of my parents buying me a car once I got my driver's license. I'd finally be free to come and go as I pleased. That dream quickly vanished with my father's declaration.

"Why did you even let me get a driver's license?" I sarcastically asked.

That outburst didn't go over well and all discussions about buying me a car instantly

stopped.

One day, I again dug in when shopping with my mother at the mall. She wanted to buy me a new pair of sunglasses.

"Why do I need sunglasses? It's not like I have a car to wear them in," I said. Yep, that hole kept getting deeper and deeper.

. . .

My mother once gave me an embroidered pillow that read: "Mirror Mirror on the Wall, I've Become My Mother After All." I always laughed at the idea that I'd become my mother and swore it would never happen, until it did.

She often said, "I only hope one day you'll have a child who challenges you as much as you do me."

She got her wish.

When talking to Jack about learning to drive, I heard my mother's voice despite the fact the words were mine.

"I'm not worried about you driving; it's the other person."

To add to this sense of déjà vu, whenever I used this rationale, Jack rolled his eyes at me precisely as I did when my mother mouthed the exact words.

And then Jack said, "Mom, I've got to learn some time, and it's going to be fine."

But would it be? I then heard more of my mother's words escaping my mouth.

"Well, when I was your age, we took learning to drive seriously and were better drivers."

That's not to say there weren't bad drivers, car accidents, speeding, or the occasional fender bender with my generation.

"Mom, what's the worst thing you did after you started driving?" he asked.

I've always loved Jack's ability to divert the conversation away from him and put me on the spot. I hesitated to answer immediately in fear of him holding my answer over me for years.

There were several examples to choose from, like when I drove my friend Abbe and her sister Melanie home from school and fishtailed into someone's yard, nearly running into a tree. Or the time I again drove Abbe and Melanie home, and as I pulled my car into their driveway, the car wouldn't stop so I had to slam the brakes to keep from crashing into their garage. (Recalling these incidents now makes me believe the bad luck common denominator wasn't my inexperienced driving skills but Abbe and Melanie.)

"Once, I was backing out of a friend's driveway and didn't see the car parked across the street and hit it. Instead of doing the right thing and leaving a note letting the car's owner know what I did, I drove off," I told him.

He looked at me with wide eyes as I continued.

"I thought it was over until my friend's mother told the neighbor who hit his car and gave him my phone number. He called my dad to determine whether we would pay for the damage. And I wasn't allowed to drive for a month."

Truth: I'm a much better driver today than when I was sixteen, especially since nearly failing my driver's test.

Unlike my generation, today's teenagers aren't in a hurry to get their driver's licenses. What was once considered a ticket to freedom is now replaced with Uber and Lyft. And if you live in a major city like New York, getting around via subway, bus, or train is even easier. According to the Federal Highway Administration, more than 42 percent of sixteen-year-olds had driver's licenses in 1993. By 2021, that number had dropped to just 25 percent.

Jack will eventually drive a car after proper training to ensure he's less likely to trench a yard or take out a tree during his road test, as I almost did. He'll also get a job to pay for the absorbent car insurance and gasoline, like I did. I'll age a lifetime and frequent my hair colorist going through the process. But like my parents, I'll survive.

As parents of teenagers, we're nearing the end of our days of influence. They'll be off to college and the working world in the blink of an eye. We can only hope that our love, guidance, advice, and constant badgering throughout their lives will have impacted their future selves. And if we're lucky, they'll take a little piece of us with them—like being a neat freak, enjoying the love of great classic rock music, and having good driving skills—and one day share it all with their teenage children, who hopefully will challenge them too.

Stuck in the Middle

POCWAM

WHEN YOU HAVE A child in your forties, your parents are also older. My parents were seventy-three when Jack was born. But they were a young seventy-three. They loved playing golf, cruising, and living their best lives.

"Your life is busier than mine," I told my mother. "You're never home."

But even with their fun, busy lives, the reality was like me being an older mother: my parents were older grandparents.

"You better have a child while I'm still able to sit on the floor and play with them and get up without breaking my hip," my mother always half-joked.

"The same thought goes for me," I'd tell her.

. . .

Unfortunately, living in New York with parents who lived in Florida didn't provide me with the luxury of having family close by to help me care for Jack. In the summer of 2008, our nanny, Christina, took a week's vacation. Because Adam and I worked full-time, I had to get creative with childcare. I decided to call my mom.

"Mama, can you come to New York for the week? I need help with Jack while the nanny is on vacation."

"Oh, twist my arm. Of course I'll be there. You only need me for a week?" my mom gleefully replied.

Nothing made her happier than spending time with her grandson. I booked her airline ticket, and a few days later, we picked her up from Newark Airport. On the way home, we stopped at Buy Buy Baby in New Jersey. With Jack barely nine months old, we needed an adjustable fence for the living room to keep him safe from grabbing breakables off the bookshelves as he crawled around the floor. We found what we believed to be the perfect solution, but the minute we unpacked the fence, we knew it was a POCWOM, or Piece of Crap, Waste of Money. Adam and I coined the acronym after buying and getting rid of many useless, must-have baby-related items all our friends swore we needed.

"My kids loved the mechanical swing, and every time they cried, I put them in it, and they stopped crying," said Melinda, my best friend and go-to expert on motherhood. So, we bought one for Jack. Unfortunately, the swing only made him cry harder. We immediately gave it away, and the POCWAM was born. In just nine months, we amassed a vast collection of POCWAMs, and like most new parents, the list kept growing and is still going strong today.

After unpacking the fence, we placed Jack on the floor where he immediately started wailing.

"He looks like he's in baby jail and is trying to break out," I shouted over his screams.

"He's going to climb over that fence in no time," my mother said.

"Back to Buy Buy Baby," Adam added with a sigh.

As the three of us sat around watching Jack try to break free from baby prison, my mom's cell phone rang.

"Yes, this is Barbara. What? Is he okay?" we heard her nervously say to whoever was on the phone. "I see. Yes, I just arrived at Judy's, but I'll get a reservation to come home tomorrow."

I wasn't sure what was happening, but I knew it had to do with my father. Only horrible thoughts raced through my mind.

"Mama, what's wrong with Daddy? Is he okay?" I asked her as she hung up the phone.

"Your father was having dinner at the country club and fell in the dining room. He's hurt, and the ambulance took him to the hospital. I need to fly back to Florida."

I stood frozen in disbelief.

"I hate leaving you by yourself with no one to stay with Jack. I feel terrible. But I need to go home and care for your father."

"Mama, you must go home and take care of Daddy. He needs you, and I'll be fine," I reassured her.

As much as I needed my mother, my father needed her more. He was alone and scared, and her worrying the entire time would do us no good. This incident officially made me a card-carrying member of the sandwich generation, stuck in the middle of caring for my son and worrying about the well-being of my parents.

My mother left the following day. As soon as she got back to Florida, I called her.

"How's Daddy? Is he home from the hospital yet?" I asked.

"He's home. He swears he tripped over something but doesn't remember anything except being embarrassed by falling in front of people. I'm so sorry I had to leave you so quickly. I feel terrible."

"No need to feel that way. It's not the end of the world, and Christina will be back next week. If we can't handle one week without help, how will we ever figure out the rest of Jack's life?"

For the remainder of the week, Adam and I were like two ships that passed at night. I'd take the morning shift, then Adam would come home from his office and take the afternoon shift while I went into the office. Even though Adam and I made it all work, my thoughts never left my father's health or my mother's well-being.

"I hate that I'm not with you to take care of Daddy. You do so much for him and need a break," I said.

"I'll be fine," Mom told me.

My mother always told me this—no matter the situation—to not worry me. I never truly believed her words, though. Being smack in the middle of the sandwich generation, with no siblings to help shoulder any burdens that might come my way, and having a toddler and a full-time job, made life feel overwhelming. But life happens, as they say. This was the reality of being an older mom with older parents.

Fortunately, my dad rallied, leaving me believing he was on borrowed time. Regardless, I was so thankful he was around to know his grandson.

Do We Get Frequent Flier Miles?

FOR JACK'S FIRST BIRTHDAY, Adam, a French Culinary Institute amateur cooking school graduate, decided he would make one of his fancy cakes from scratch: a chocolate genoise cake with chocolate ganache icing.

"Are you sure you want to make such a fancy cake for a one-year-old?" I asked.

But I already knew the answer. Adam loved practicing the skills he learned from his classes, and the cake would be more for adults than babies. We decided on a fireman-themed party, and in keeping with our theme, we bought a fire truck cake pan. After Adam measured and mixed all the ingredients with the precision of a scientist in a lab, he poured the batter into the pan. Unfortunately, not even a Nobel Prize for Science winner could have predicted the messy blob the cake would become because of the thinness of the cake pan.

"The cake is stuck in the mold and won't come out. I'm going to have to throw it away and start over," he said.

"Can't you use icing to smush it back together?" I asked.

"Nope, the cake is too fragile for the pan and keeps falling apart," he said.

Adam made another cake using the same ingredients and techniques as the first one and, surprise, got the same result. I could feel his frustration and decided to step in.

"I'll go to the store and buy a Betty Crocker cake mix. Everyone loves Betty, and no one will know the difference."

"No, I'll make this cake work. I'll use icing to put it together," he said.

Gee, I wished I had thought of that idea. The finished cake looked beautiful, and Adam masterfully decorated it with a fire truck's colorful, intricate details.

Several family members, including my parents who had traveled from Florida, and friends attended the soiree. I loved having my mom and dad there because celebrations were the cornerstone of our family. But something about my father seemed off.

"Are you feeling okay?" I asked my dad. "You don't seem like your-self."

I couldn't quite put my finger on why I felt like he was ill.

"I'm okay. I'm just happy to be here," he assured me with a smile.

Once Jack awoke from his nap, we gathered around his high chair to sing "Happy Birthday." Adam sliced a sliver of cake and gave it to Jack. Jack didn't know what to make of the brightly colored chocolate delight on his plate, so he grabbed a handful of cake with a big blob of icing, put it to his lips, scrunched up his face, and quickly spit it out while crying.

I turned to my mother and said, "I guess he would have preferred Betty Crocker."

· · ·

My parents turned seventy-five in 2009, and to celebrate their mile-stone, that January they booked a fabulous South American cruise that set sail from São Paulo. The Sunday night before Adam and I returned to work after the Christmas holidays, I had just gotten Jack to sleep when the phone rang. I noticed it was my father's cell phone number in the caller ID. I assumed my parents were calling from Miami while waiting to board their flight to São Paulo, where they'd board the ship the following day.

"Judy, we're in Panama. Your father is in the hospital," my mother said.

I felt the blood rush to my head, and my ears started ringing.

"What? What happened?" I barely got the words out before my tears flowed.

"We were on the plane, about to land for our connecting flight, and your father started getting sick. He couldn't stop, and it was a real mess," she explained.

I sat in silence as she continued.

"The flight attendants had the captain call for an ambulance to meet the plane so we could get your father to the hospital. When we got off the plane, I had to run to a store inside the airport to get him a clean shirt. Then they took our passports, kept our luggage, and transported us to the hospital."

I kept thinking this had to be a nightmare.

"Mama, where are you now?" I asked.

"We're at the hospital, but it's a private facility, and to keep him here, I have to pay $10,000 cash," she cried.

"And what happens if you don't pay them?" I asked.

"They'll move him to a public hospital. I told them I don't have $10,000, so they're preparing to transfer him now."

So many worries filled my head, but the most significant concern was the language barrier. The thought of my mother sitting in a hospital waiting room in Panama, not knowing my father's condition, and not being able to communicate with the nurses or doctors devastated me. I had to get to her and help.

"I'm going to call your internist in Florida and have her call the hospital to find out Daddy's condition and our options to get you out of there," I said.

My parents' doctor spoke Spanish, and I knew she'd translate for me if I could reach her. The other challenge was that my mom's cell phone could only make outgoing calls. I couldn't call her; she could only contact me.

"I need you to call me every fifteen minutes to check in," I told my mom.

Fortunately, my parents' doctor was on call that night and returned my message.

"Judy, I spoke to the hospital, and they don't believe your father had a heart attack based on the initial tests they ran. They aren't able to perform an MRI due to your father's pacemaker, but he may have had a stroke," Dr. Martinez said.

"Can I get him home?" I asked.

"They won't release him right now, but I'll check back later and let you know," she replied.

In my mind, I had to get down to Panama to be with my mother. She was scared, and I was petrified. I hated the feeling of helplessness and wanted to be with my parents. But I also had to be at home for my one-year-old son.

"Adam, I need to fly to Panama in the morning," I said, frantic.

"I'm not thrilled with the thought of you flying down there yourself," he said.

"I know, but I can't leave them there. I've got to get them out of that country. And they don't even have their luggage or passports," I cried.

Adam had an idea as I paced the floor, waiting for my mom's next call.

"Doesn't one of your PR clients rescue people in war-torn countries and disaster zones all the time? Maybe they can help us get your parents out," he said.

I called my client, David, who worked for Air Partner, at that moment.

"This better be important, seeing as you're calling me late on a Sunday night," he said, teasing me.

After explaining the situation, he called an air ambulance service he worked with in Fort Lauderdale to give them a heads-up. He then contacted us to iron out the details.

"They can help you, but I'll be blunt. It's going to cost a lot of money," he said.

"I don't care what it costs. I've got to get my mom and dad home," I told him.

Adam spoke to the pilot and made all the arrangements. David wasn't joking about the cost. The fee for the air ambulance and personnel was $20,000.

"Put it on my American Express card. At least we'll get the points," Adam said.

Less than twenty-four hours after my parents arrived in Panama, an air ambulance landed, secured their passports and luggage, went to the hospital to pick them up, and flew them to the Cleveland Clinic in Fort Lauderdale. While my parents were being rescued and flown back to the States, I booked a flight to Palm Beach Airport.

"I want to take you to the airport. Can you call a babysitter to come to stay with Jack?" Adam asked.

As we waited for Lizzie, our sitter, and I packed my suitcase, I heard a loud crash, then Jack screaming from his bedroom. Adam and I ran into Jack's room and found him in the middle of shards of broken glass. He'd pulled down the poll lamp next to his changing table that we thought we'd secured. My heart stopped. What else could go wrong? Was this his way of saying *Mommy, don't leave me?* Thankfully, he didn't have a scratch on him, and Adam threw away the lamp.

I arrived at Palm Beach Airport and took a taxi to my parents' house. I picked up their car and drove to the Cleveland Clinic in Fort Lauderdale. I wasn't sure I could stop crying when I walked into the hospital and saw my mother.

"I've never been happier to see you in my life! Are you okay?" I cried.

"I am now," she said as she hugged me tight. "Thank you for getting us home. How much will this cost?"

"Don't worry about it right now. But we're going to be able to take a fabulous vacation on points," I joked.

Fortunately, my mother had purchased trip insurance with the cruise package, so we later got our money back. With this news, I felt like we had won the lottery.

When I finally walked into my father's room, I tried to make a pithy, sarcastic comment that I knew would make him laugh. But the only thing I could think of was "Are you kidding me?"

The doctor met with my mother and me and told us that he hadn't had a heart attack. Like the doctors had said in Panama, they couldn't give him an MRI to determine whether he had a stroke because of his pacemaker. The truth: they didn't know what had happened to explain why he got so sick on the airplane. But then the doctor hit us with a gut punch.

"Your husband has dementia," he said.

We blankly stared at him.

"What?" we both replied.

"I asked him a series of questions about what happened, and he couldn't recall most of it. It appears early, but I'd like to do more tests on him. Have you noticed any signs of forgetfulness?"

"I have noticed signs of him forgetting things here and there, but no more than usual. He recently decided to stop driving, but I thought it was because he hasn't been sturdy on his feet. Are you sure?" my mother asked.

"Don't you think he's in shock from the entire ordeal, and that's why he doesn't remember anything?" I asked.

"I won't know until I do more tests, but I'm afraid I'm right," the doctor said.

My dad's dementia diagnosis hit me hard but gave me clarity on the definition of sandwich generation. I felt sandwiched between helping my mom with my dad and rushing home to care for my one-year-old son, husband, and job. Honestly, I'm not a fan of a sandwich unless it's a good PB&J. In addition to its taste, this childhood staple represents easier times when my most complicated decisions centered on crunchy or smooth peanut butter, Skippy or Jif, and grape or strawberry jelly. If life could only be that simple.

The Sandwich Generation

MY DAD HAD OVERCOME many health challenges, from hemophilia to hepatitis to heart disease to cancer, but he'd always bounced back. In January 2009, he was diagnosed with dementia. The diagnosis felt like none of his previous ailments. It felt so final. I understood he could have succumbed to any of his illnesses, but he knew what was happening to him and could fight. Dementia robbed him of his ability to fight.

My father stood six foot four and was a very confident and proud man. His work ethic and appreciation of life's simple pleasures were contagious and something I always wanted to mimic. He never wanted to be a burden and seldom asked anyone for anything.

"My worst nightmare is relying on others to care for me," he often said. "And I never want to end up in a nursing home. Please don't put me in one."

Watching him fade away was heartbreaking. But watching what it did to my mom was unbearable. And being an only child living in another state brought me so much guilt and anxiety.

Should I rush to my mom's side to help her care for my father or stay home to care for my toddler?

If you looked up the definition of "sandwich generation" in the dictionary, my picture sat next to the description. I felt like the turkey, cheese, and lettuce between two halves of a poppyseed Kaiser roll.

Before my father left the Cleveland Clinic, where he'd been for a week, my mother and I had to find a skilled nursing facility for him to receive physical therapy. He was becoming less steady on his feet, and the doctor thought getting him some extra support before he went home would help strengthen his legs. My mom and I visited several facilities, one worse than the next. We knew this wasn't going to make my father happy.

"Why are places like this so depressing and have to smell?" I asked my mom.

She stared at me as if to say "You have to ask?"

We selected a skilled nursing facility in Boca Raton, about thirty minutes from my parents' house in Boynton Beach. Fortunately, it would be temporary until my father gained more strength to come home. A few days later, after my father entered the facility, I had to return to New York for my job, family, and life. I hated leaving my mom to drive back and forth to Boca, but I had no choice.

"I'll be back as soon as possible," I told my mom when she dropped me off at the airport. My tears flowed hard, and the guilt strangled me.

. . .

In January 2010, a year after my father's dementia diagnosis, I walked into my apartment after an early morning workout session. Adam met me at the door.

"Your dad fell out of bed and broke his hip. He's scheduled for surgery today," he said.

My father had been in the hospital for several days because of pneumonia. He was scheduled to go home that day. I stood there in tears as Adam held me. We didn't need to say a word because we both knew. This moment was the beginning of the end and what I called the "long goodbye." My father's worst nightmare had come true. Any ounce of independence he had was now gone.

I found myself in a familiar habit of rushing to Florida. I wanted to bring Jack with me, but I wouldn't have anyone to care for him as I shuttled my mother back and forth to the hospital. Fortunately, Jack was cared for by Adam, nannies, and babysitters I had on call. But I also had my job. I had to call my boss.

"Allen, my father fell out of bed in the hospital and broke his hip. I'm on my way to Florida, but I'll take work with me, so everything gets done."

"Judy, we understand. Go be with your mom and dad and keep us posted," he said.

I worked for incredible people who had experienced aging parents. Helen, Allen, and Carolyn, my employers, and owners of Vollmer Public Relations, were empathetic and allowed me to spend time with my father while helping my mother get her affairs in order.

I flew to Florida that afternoon, and by the time I arrived at the hospital, my father was out of surgery.

"How did it go?" I asked my mom when she picked me up from the airport. "Is Daddy going to be okay?"

"The surgery went well. But he can't come home. I can't take care of him by myself anymore."

While my father recovered in the hospital, my mother and I searched for a skilled nursing facility with physical therapy. I couldn't get my father's words about never wanting to be in a nursing home out of my head. I felt like we were betraying him. But he needed around-the-clock care, and my mother couldn't help him alone.

We decided on an assisted living facility in Delray Beach, just a short drive from their home in Boynton Beach. By April, the facility told my mother she needed to find another place with a memory care unit. His cognitive ability worsened, and they no longer had the capabilities to help him. I once again flew to Florida to help my mother find a new living community for my father. This time I took Jack and our wonderful nanny, Desirée, with me. Desirée didn't know that besides caring for Jack, her presence also supported my mom and me.

On this trip, Jack learned to climb out of his portable bed. One night, while I was in a deep sleep from sheer exhaustion, I felt someone staring at me and then felt someone touch my cheek.

"Oh my gosh!" I screamed as I opened my eyes. "How did you get here?"

Jack stood looking directly at me while stroking my face. We moved the portable bed into Desirée's room the next night.

After viewing several memory care facilities, my mom and I found a small one that we liked. The Cottages was less than fifteen minutes from her house. The buildings were painted yellow, and the rooms were bright and didn't smell. The staff members were friendly and treated everyone with respect and kindness, preserving whatever dignity the residents had left. It takes a particular person to work in a place like this. But it was still depressing.

Life can be cruel at times, especially as we age. My father had recently celebrated his seventy-sixth birthday. Still, he was among the youngest people in his memory care unit. I had a hard time dealing with that fact.

When it came time for me to return to New York, I cried, but not just for me. I cried for my mother, yes, but my tears flowed harder for my father. I hated leaving him in a place like this, even with its cheery surroundings and friendly workers. Gone was his smile, sarcasm, spark for life, and will to live. As I said my goodbyes, it felt like a knife pierced my heart. My mind rushed like a Ping-Pong ball bouncing between feelings of despair for my mother and heartache for my father. The only silver lining, as much as I could call it, was that my father probably didn't understand much of what was happening to him.

I hated that my father wouldn't be around to see Jack grow into the young man I knew he'd be proud of. I hated that my father was leaving my mother when they had so much more living to do. I kept reminding myself that because I had a child later in life, my parents were older too. I knew this, but no matter how much I tried to trick my mind into accepting the reality, my heart wasn't ready to say goodbye.

. . .

My father's health declined rapidly, and by October 2010, he was in the hospital again. One afternoon, while I was at work, my mom called me from the hospital.

"I'm here with a hospice nurse to speak about options for Daddy," she said.

"Hospice?" I asked. "Does this mean we're at the end?"

My experience with hospice was with my sister at the end of her life. I always thought people placed their loved ones in hospice to keep them comfortable right before they died. Since I knew my father's health had been quickly declining, it didn't surprise me that we were here, but I still had a hard time hearing it.

"I'm going to put the nurse on the phone to explain things to you," my mother said.

"Hello, Judy. What questions do you have for me?" she asked.

"How much longer do you think he has?" I asked.

"Hospice isn't just for end of life. We concentrate on palliative care and quality of life support," she said.

"Does that mean he's not about to die?"

"It's hard to say, but he's not eating, so he can't sustain much longer. He may have several weeks, even months; we just don't know."

She handed the phone to my mom.

"I think you should come now," she said.

"I'll be there tomorrow," I replied.

I packed up my desk, bringing as much work as I could do remotely. I didn't know how long I'd be in Florida.

My mom picked me up at the airport the following day, and we went directly to the hospital. I walked into my father's room, and as soon as he saw me, he sat straight up in bed with the biggest smile.

"Judy, you came! I'm so glad you're here."

I couldn't believe it. I thought my dad would look like Celia the day she died. I'll never forget what I saw the morning I walked into her hospital room. What laid in the bed was a shell of a woman with pasty gray skin that looked nothing like the sister I'd known. I expected my dad to look the same. Instead, he looked like he wanted to jump out of bed and hug me. If only he could have done that.

My father remained a few more nights in the hospital before returning to the Cottages. A rabbi visited him a few days later. I sat with my father as he spoke to the rabbi.

"Robert, can you tell me what's happening in this picture?" the rabbi asked, pointing to pictures my mother had brought to decorate the room.

"Oh, that's from my wedding, and that's my wife, Barbara," he said with a smile.

He proceeded to tell the rabbi about his wedding day. "The wedding was a big affair, and the whole town of Wharton attended. Barbara and I didn't know half the people, but it was a great time."

Then the rabbi asked who the little girls were in another picture.

"Those are *my* girls," he said, beaming. "That one is Celia, and the other one is Judy."

And then he grabbed my hand. I wiped a tear from his face.

Dementia robbed him of fighting to live, but it never robbed him of remembering his family. That brought so much comfort to me.

Later that evening, back at my mother's house, I sat with her to discuss the inevitable.

"I know this will be hard, but I think we should make funeral arrangements while I'm here, so if I'm not with you when the time comes, you won't have to scramble, and you won't be alone," I told my mom.

"I agree," she said with tears in her eyes.

Coordinating funeral arrangements ranks as one of the worst tasks you'll ever do, especially when the person is still alive. But I knew this was the right time.

The next day, we brought my father's tallis, a prayer shawl, to the funeral home. According to Jewish death rituals and law, the deceased can rest wearing a simple white shroud in addition to their tallis.

"Do you have any children?" the funeral coordinator asked me.

"Yes, I have a son who is almost three years old," I said.

She cut a few tassels from my father's tallis and handed them to me.

"When your son becomes a bar mitzvah, you can incorporate these tassels into the ceremony," she said.

My mother and I sat and cried together. At that moment, as I held the tassels in my hand, I knew my father would always be with Jack.

Joy and Sadness

THANKSGIVING OF 2010, Jack's third birthday, and my parent's fifty-fourth wedding anniversary fell on the same day. By November, my father's health was in a steady decline, but I still felt I had a lot to be thankful for in my life that year. My mother struggled with whether to leave my father in order to come to New York to be with Adam, Jack, and me for the holiday and Jack's birthday. The thought of her by herself over the holiday upset me. Even though her world was crumbling under the weight of my father's illness, she deserved happiness.

"Mama, I think Daddy will be fine for a few days while you come to New York to be with us," I told her. "I know the guilt you're feeling for leaving him because I have similar feelings, but I know Daddy would want you to be with family."

"I know, but I'm so torn and can't bear leaving him," she cried.

Truth: I'm not sure my father would have noticed her absence. My heart broke for my mom.

Ultimately, my mother came to New York, and we celebrated all the festivities at my friend Hannah's house. Thanksgiving, and every holiday, is always a big affair at Hannah's, and this meal was no different. She had a lot of people and tons of food; it was just what the doctor had ordered for all of us.

. . .

The week after Thanksgiving, while sitting at work, I received a call from my cousin Fred.

"I'm going to tell you something, but you have to promise not to tell anyone, especially Kay. If she finds out, I'll know it was you," he said.

"Okay, I promise, I guess," I said hesitantly.

Fred and Kay are my cousins, and Jack's godparents, but so much more. They've been there for every significant moment in my life and beyond, and I'm not sure where I'd be without their guidance and loving support. No matter the ask, I'd do anything for either of them.

"You're going to get a call from Andy, Leslie's boyfriend, and he needs a favor," he said.

"And what favor does he need?" I cautiously asked.

"He's bringing Leslie to New York to propose, and he wants you and Adam to help him select the perfect location," he said.

"Oh my gosh!" I squealed with excitement. "We're on it!"

There was a running joke among Leslie, Fred and Kay's eldest child, and her siblings—Mark, Jay, and Nancy—about whether she'd wait as long as I did to get married. At this time, Leslie was thirty-two, and while that's not old maid territory, it's later than most girls in Texas get married. I'd always hoped to be a role model for my cousins, but I prayed they'd tie the knot and have children earlier than I did.

"Do you have any ideas of where you want to propose?" I asked when Andy called me.

"Anywhere but the tree at Rockefeller Center," he said. "It's too many people and too obvious."

We decided on Central Park. Adam took his camera, scouted different locations around the park, and sent pictures to Andy to let him decide. He ultimately selected a little pavilion next to the iconic Bow Bridge. The plan was for Adam and me to hide near where he proposed and take pictures. Once he asked her, and she said yes, he'd point to us, and we'd join them. It was going to be perfect.

And then my father's health took a turn for the worse.

The afternoon before the engagement would take place, my mother called me.

"Judy, it won't be long now," my mom said, crying.

"Should I fly out tonight?" I asked her.

She wasn't sure so she put the doctor on the phone.

"We never know how much longer a person has, but your father's organs are beginning to shut down. My best guess is that he has a few days at most," the doctor said.

I sat on the phone, paralyzed with conflicting emotions swirling in my heart. I needed to rush to my father to say goodbye (even though I'd said my goodbyes the last time I saw him). Still, I desperately wanted to be in the city for Leslie's engagement.

"Mama, what you don't know is that Leslie is getting engaged tomorrow morning, and we're in on the surprise," I said. "You can't tell Kay, or Fred will know I told you!"

"Oh, how wonderful. I promise I won't say anything," she said.

"If you think I need to get there right away, I'll find a flight tonight, but if you think there's a chance I can wait until tomorrow, please let me know," I said.

"The doctor thinks he has a little more time, so please stay and enjoy this special moment. I know your father would want you there for Leslie."

. . .

The December morning was frigid, with temperatures hovering in the teens. I met my trainer, Jenny, in Central Park near the proposal site to hand off Jack for a few hours. She had agreed to babysit for the morning.

"Please take him away from this spot. The last thing I need is for him to spoil the surprise," I said.

Adam and I took our place on a hill behind a tree and waited. And waited. And waited some more. Every few minutes, I'd get a text from Andy.

She keeps stopping to look at everything in the park. But I promise we're on our way.

Then I'd get a text from Fred.

What is taking so long? Kay is getting suspicious.

It felt like a covert operation, with me in the middle feeding information to both sides.

Finally, Andy and Leslie emerged. And not a minute too soon because I swear, I'd lost feeling in my extremities from the subzero windchill. The proposal was flawless, and Leslie was shocked, especially when she turned around to see Adam and me standing on the hill taking pictures. Smiles and happiness surrounded everyone, and I felt a sense of calmness and peace for just a moment. I held on to these emotions for as long as possible, knowing what lay ahead in a few hours.

"He survived the night, but it won't be much longer," my mom told me. "He's stopped eating and isn't responding much."

"Okay, we leave this evening. Please tell Daddy I'm on my way."

This conversation felt like déjà vu from the time I rushed to Celia's side before she died. I remember saying the same thing to my mom about telling Celia to hang on until I could get there to say goodbye.

The scramble to get to Florida during the week of Christmas was chaotic. Adam and I already had flights booked for later in the week, but fortunately, we found three seats on a JetBlue flight leaving that night. We quickly packed and rushed to JFK Airport. The whole process was a blur, but I remember struggling with what dress to wear to the funeral.

My father had been a sharp-dressed man and had always had a comment about my attire, no matter the occasion. If I wore inappropriate clothing, or at least what he believed to be questionable, I almost certainly got sent back to my room to change outfits. But as critical as he had been about my attire, he'd always told me when I looked nice, like the day of Celia's funeral when I came downstairs to get in the limo.

"Judy, you look very pretty, and I know Celia would think so too," he said.

I had to look pretty for him.

I also had to pack for Jack, a much easier endeavor. While he knew we were going to Florida and was excited to play outside and swim in Grammy and Papa's pool, he didn't know about the inevitable side trip to Houston. He was three, so I wasn't sure how I would explain it, or if he would even understand.

Our plane touched down at about 10:30 p.m. at the Palm Beach airport. Adam drove me directly to the Cottages so I could spend time with my father.

"I'll be back with your mom as soon as we get Jack settled with the neighbor. Hang in there," Adam said.

"I'll try," I said.

I walked into my father's room, where an aide sat with him while watching *Keeping Up with the Kardashians*. I'd never watched an episode of this program before, so she began telling me about the different

Kardashian family members. I told her she could keep watching if she wanted to. Instead, she turned off the television and left the room so I could spend quiet time with my father. I crawled into his bed beside him and placed my head on his chest. I don't know if he knew I was there, but I prayed he did so he could hear what I said.

"Daddy, it's time for you to go to sleep. I know you're worried about leaving Mommy and me, but you're so tired, and we can no longer be selfish about wanting you to stay here. I am the luckiest daughter in the world, having you as my father. I cannot imagine my life without you and your guidance, but know you've done everything you could to teach me and make me a better person. I'm sorry for all my actions that made you angry and how I sarcastically talked back to you. But hey, I learned everything from the master: you! I'm so happy you lived to know Adam and meet your grandson, Jack. I hate you won't be here to watch him grow up, but he'll know everything about you, especially how you loved him. I love you so much, and I will miss everything about you. I'll always be your little girl, and you'll be in my heart forever. Please tell Celia I miss and love her every day, and thank her for giving me the years I had with you that she didn't get. You're all hers now. Please watch over us, and I know I'll see you again one day."

He didn't respond, but as I held his hand, I swore I felt him try to squeeze mine. I'll never know if that was real, but I'll hold on to that feeling forever.

Shortly after, Adam and my mother entered the room. My mom and I just held each other tight. It was getting late, and we needed to leave. Before we left, I gave my cell phone number to a nurse.

"Please call me no matter what time if anything happens. We'll immediately come back if needed," I told her.

She agreed, and we left.

When we got to my mother's house, we stood in her foyer, speaking to her neighbor, Pauline, who had come over to stay with Jack. As my mother walked Pauline to the door, thanking her for staying at the house, she fell and banged up her knee.

"Get in the bathroom so I can clean you up," I said. "That cut looks nasty."

While cleaning my mom's knee, Adam entered the bathroom and handed me my cell phone.

"Judy, it's the nurse," he said.

I stared at Adam with hesitation but finally took the phone.

"Hello," I said. "Is my father gone?"

"No, sweetie. But you need to come back. It's time."

My mother and I quickly jumped in the car and sped to the Cottages. I'm confident I broke every traffic law, including running multiple red lights.

By the time we entered his room, it was too late.

"He's gone," the nurse said. "It happened after we hung up the phone."

"He pushed me," my mother said.

"What? Who pushed you?" I asked.

"In the foyer. Your father didn't want me to see him die, so he pushed me down."

"That's a horrible thing to think. Daddy would never push you."

"He'd never do it on purpose. It was just a way of distracting me so I would be thinking of something else when he was dying."

While my mom held on to that thought, all I could think was that, like my sister before she passed, he'd waited for me to say goodbye. And I'd hold on to that forever.

No More Airplanes!

LOSING A PARENT differs from losing a sibling. When my sister, Celia, died at twenty-six, I mourned for the life she would never experience. Sitting with her as she took her last breath, I felt like I, at the tender age of nineteen, had died too. My anger toward the life she'd never live became part of my grief. I vowed to keep living for her and me.

When my father died, while I was an adult woman at forty-six years old, I felt like a frightened little girl. I worried about my life without the one person who protected me from all the scary things. My daddy had died, and I couldn't fathom the thought of him being gone or my life without him. But while my grief consumed me, I couldn't help but think about how different I felt compared to losing my sister and how fortunate I was to have my father in my life for so long.

Grief is personal, and no two people experience it the same. I'm sure experts would say losing a sister so young in life can't compare to losing a father who lived a longer life. While that may be true, for me, the experience of losing my father while in the throes of my career, marriage, and raising a toddler meant I didn't allow myself to grieve. I didn't have the time.

The PR agency I worked for had recently been sold, and I was now a part-time employee. I was resentful, hurt, bitter, and ready to move on. Or these feelings manifested as my grief. I couldn't imagine leaving a job and career I'd worked so hard to build. But Jack was now three, and I felt I was missing everything. While I had a wonderful nanny supporting me, I wanted to raise Jack. I was so torn with what to do. Plus, my father had died.

Between work responsibilities and Jack, when was I supposed to grieve?

The whirlwind of activity following my father's passing is a blur. Fortunately, since my mother and I had coordinated everything with the funeral home ahead of time, we only needed to book our flights to Houston as the funeral service would be in Texas.

Because of the Christmas holiday week, our flight choices were limited.

"The only available flights this evening leave from Miami with four seats in first class," Adam said.

"Well, my father would only want the best for us. Book them," I said.

The funeral home arranged for my father's remains to be transported from Florida to Texas on the same flight. In a weird, surreal way, knowing my father was with us brought me comfort. It felt as if we were bringing him home.

. . .

Our family burial plot is at the Shearith Israel Cemetery in Wharton, Texas, approximately sixty miles south of Houston. This was my family's synagogue growing up. Seeing so many friends travel to Wharton from Houston for the funeral humbled me. My father had loved my friends; I knew he'd have been glad they were there for me.

We buried my father next to my sister. While consumed with grief, my heart was whole, knowing Celia was waiting for him on the other side. When Celia died, her only request was to find a pretty spot for her to rest. The cemetery in Wharton has few trees, but the area my parents selected has an oversized oak tree to shade our family plot. "This way, it will shade Celia in the hot Texas sun," my parents said. "Only the best for Bubela." Bubela was the Yiddish nickname given to Celia by our papa, meaning darling or sweetie. By contrast, Papa called me Bondit, Yiddish for pain in the neck.

"Look, she's waiting for him," I told my mother, pointing to Celia's headstone.

The plot holds four spaces, and my mother put my father right next to Celia. "At least he won't be alone."

"I'm sure she'll talk his head off when she sees him," my mother said, laughing.

"She has so much lost time to make up," I said.

The rabbi's eulogy was meaningful and brought us all comfort. After the service, it was difficult for me to leave the cemetery. I felt like I was leaving a huge piece of me behind. But we had to get back to Houston to pick up Jack. Because he was so young, he hadn't come to the cemetery with us. Instead, he'd stayed at my friend Melinda's house with her housekeeper.

Later that evening, we sat shiva at my cousins Kay and Fred's house. It was hard to believe that just a few days earlier, we had all celebrated their daughter Leslie and her fiancé Andy's engagement, and now we were gathered for my father's funeral. Such is the circle of life.

Shiva is the mourning period after the funeral service, lasting seven days. Each night, a service called a minyan is led by a rabbi in the house of mourning. Family and friends come together to help the grieving family heal and get a free meal since food is always the centerpiece of any Jewish gathering.

So many of my parents' friends, and my friends, joined us. While I loved seeing everyone, I hated the occasion. Fortunately, Jack entertained the crowd with his cute and funny personality. He had no idea what was happening, and honestly, that was okay.

My mother, Adam, Jack, and I flew back to Florida the following day. Because my mother felt more comfortable in her home, we finished the shiva for my father at her house.

"I hate that we're leaving you," I told her the morning we left Florida to go back to New York. "I'm going to call you every day."

"And I'll pick up the phone. You are my strength, and I love you so much," she said.

We stood there, hugging each other through tears. Neither one of us wanted to let go.

Jack started getting upset as we drove to the Palm Beach airport's rental car return center. At first, I thought his sadness was leaving his Grammy, but I was wrong.

"Mommy, no airplane. No more airplanes," he cried.

While dealing with the grief of losing my father and being busy making all the funeral and travel arrangements, I forgot how this must have felt to Jack. He didn't know why we'd schlepped him back and forth from New York to Florida to Texas and back to Florida. By the end, he'd had enough.

I tried my hardest to shield my sorrow from Jack. I'm sure he felt my sadness, though. Kids know. Occasionally, he'd say, "Mommy, don't cry." And then he'd wipe my tears. I didn't have time to grieve for my dad.

When we got to the ticket counter at the airport, we learned the airline had canceled our flight because of a snowstorm on the East Coast that had shut down the New York airports.

"Your only option is to fly to Boston," the ticket agent told us. "I can get you three seats on a flight leaving tomorrow."

"I guess we get to add one more airport to Jack's adventure," I said to Adam.

We returned to my mom's house and spent the night.

"I knew you'd come back," my mother said with a smile.

The following day, we landed at Boston's Logan Airport and rented a car to drive home to New York. Fortunately, Boston is a straight shot on I-95, but the roads were a mess because of the snowstorm.

"Are we ever going to get home?" I whined as we crawled along the interstate. "And I just remembered we have no food in the refrigerator."

Because we'd left New York in a hurry to get to Florida over two weeks before, we threw out most of our food. As tired as we were, we decided to stop at Whole Foods in Darien, Connecticut, on the way home.

"Planes, trains, automobiles, and grocery stores should be the theme of this travel adventure," I said.

But tomorrow was a brand-new day.

A Dance with My Father

I WROTE A TRIBUTE TO my father after he died. I wanted to speak at the funeral, but I didn't; I was too sad. If I had been able to talk, these words would have been how I remembered him. And I know he would have loved everything I had to say.

Bob Haveson. Robert Haveson. Robert Haverson, Haaverson, Havenson, Haavenson, or Mr. H.A. Veson. Through the years, my father has had many names, or at least people have tried to give him so many. No matter what anyone called him, there were several names he would forever be proud to have: son, brother, husband, uncle, father, father-in-law, Papa, and friend.

Growing up in Bayonne, New Jersey, Robert and his friends were "street kids." I always took great interest in learning of his mischievous ways as a kid because the more I understood, the more I reminded him that I was just like him. Gilbert Surpin was my father's childhood best friend. They formed a company in high school called Haveson & Surpin Truancy Specialists. They had business cards and furnished excuses to classmates, helping them escape trouble. They even gave special rates for large groups.

That sense of humor continued throughout my father's life. It translated into years of always being on guard and not falling prey to his teasing, something my mother, sister, and I often did. Not me as much. I had his number, and he knew it.

After leaving Bayonne, he joined the US Air Force during the Korean War. Oh, but don't worry, he didn't sit on the front lines or in harm's way; that might have meant his hands would have gotten dirty, something he hated more than anything. But he honorably served his country, and when stationed at Bergstrom Air Force Base in Austin, Texas, he met someone who would change his life forever: a rabbi. That rabbi introduced him to my mother. As the story goes, she attended the University of Texas at Austin, and the rabbi decided he would make a match. Of course, my father's version of the story says my mom stood him up for their first meeting, and according to him, it's a wonder they ever got together. My dad was a stickler with promptness, and after waiting for ten minutes, he left. Regardless of the real story, the two got together and shared fifty-four beautiful years.

As in most marriages, there were good days, sad days, bad days, and those days for simply making memories. But no matter what kind of day they had, their love over the past fifty-four years has always been my guiding light. Their marriage taught me there's always a way to work things out, no matter the situation. My mother's courage during my father's final days was unlike anything I could imagine. Whether he could express it, I know my father felt comforted.

Their marriage also produced two daughters. Celia Hannah arrived nine months after they married, and the other daughter (me) came seven years later, on the exact day (August 17).

Behind every good man is a strong woman, or so they say. In our household, my poor father was severely out-gendered. I'm sure he wished I had been a boy. That might be why there are pictures of us dressed alike, why I often got hand-me-downs of his belts and other clothing items, and why he always took me around like his little buddy to the car wash and the barber. It made no difference to me as I wouldn't have had it any other way.

While the sorrow of losing my father is only beginning, I'm comforted that his pain is gone. Rest well, Daddy. I love you forever.

. . .

A few years after my father died, I watched one of those singing competitions on TV. One of the male performers gave a gut-wrenching performance of Luther Vandross's "Dance with My Father." It brought tears to my eyes, but to be fair, I typically cry during insurance commercials and anything with dogs. But it made me remember my last dance with my father.

As a little girl, I loved watching my parents dance together. With my dad's six-foot-four height, dancing came effortlessly for him as he expertly led my mother across the floor. I'd stand on his feet as he tried to teach me to dance as well.

And we would always have music on in our house, especially Benny Goodman, Duke Ellington, Ella Fitzgerald, and Ol' Blue Eyes, Frank Sinatra, just to name a few. My father was always happy when he had his music playing and was dancing.

Whenever I thought about getting married, it was never the wedding dress or cake I dreamed about. Most important to me was the band and a playlist filled with many of my dad's favorites so we could have fun dancing together. For the father–daughter dance, we selected "The Way You Look Tonight." I'm not sure who was more emotional.

"I've waited forever to have this dance with you," I told him.

"You want to stand on my feet?" he asked with a smile.

My father glided me across the floor like he'd always done with my mom, and I only stepped on his foot once. But he didn't care.

We spend so much of our lives wanting this and that, and we sometimes forget to count little blessings. While sadly, I'll never have another dance with my father, I'm so fortunate to have had that last dance at my wedding, and it will be a memory I take with me forever. I only hope I'm around (and not using a walker) when Jack gets married so I can dance with him too.

When Your Parents Lose Their Independence, So Do You

SHORTLY AFTER MY FATHER died, my focus turned to my mom. Would she be okay on her own? Should I move her closer to me? Would she be happy remaining in Florida? What would she do now without my father? When I posed these questions to my mother, she knew what she wanted to do.

"I think I want to stay in Florida," she said. "I'm comfortable and have friends here, and I'm not sure I want to make a big move right now."

"You can move to New York to be closer to us. But I'm not sure how you'd like the cold winters," I said.

"There's a reason people from New York who live in Florida during the winter are called snowbirds," she joked.

I would have loved for her to move up to New York to be closer to me, but winters can be harsh for people with thin blood used to living in a warm climate.

My mother sat in her den one afternoon going through the mounds of papers and files in the drawers of my father's desk. As she picked up each piece of paper, I could see fear in her eyes.

"I'm worried about how to manage now that your father is gone. I never realized how much I relied on him," she said.

"Adam and I will help you. Please don't worry," I said.

"But I don't want to take advantage of you."

"When you're taking advantage of me, I'll let you know," I replied.

At seventy-six, my mother was alone for the first time in fifty-four years. Seeing her scared and worried about managing life alone was very unsettling. My mother's resilience through family trauma, illness, and death kept me grounded. Seeing her feeling lost petrified me.

She stayed in Florida after my father's death and remained there for twelve years. We took her with us on vacations, flew her to New York, and visited her in Florida as often as possible. I still felt guilty not being more present for her, though.

. . .

Many years after my father passed away and as my mother aged, I became concerned about her isolation, especially living far away.

Being a fiercely independent woman, she hated relying on anyone. However, I still worried, especially the summer she visited me in New York. After witnessing a steady decline in her mobility, I said, "Mama, I think it's time for you to consider a different living situation."

Imagine my surprise when she responded with a few simple words: "Okay, I'm ready."

Even though I did a little victory dance in my mind, knowing how fortunate I was that she barely resisted me, the outcome was still bittersweet. When your parents lose some of their independence, so do you. You never want to admit either of you is aging, and the older they get, the more you worry.

When the time comes for your parents to transition to a new living environment, you tend to take on the same responsibilities and tasks they did for you. And there's no more enormous task than packing and moving a lifetime of memories. This especially holds when, like me, you're an only child, and there's no one there to shoulder the heartache with you.

"Do you want to stay in Florida and look for an independent living space here? There's no shortage of options for you in South Florida," I said.

"I think I want to stay in Florida. Where else would I go?"

We'd settled on Florida until my cousin, Mark, from Houston called me with a different idea.

"Judy, why doesn't your mom move home?" Mark asked me. "She'll be with family and friends here."

"Well, if she does go to Houston, she'll be your responsibility. Are you sure you're up for this?" I said as a joke.

After we decided on Houston, Melinda, a top real estate broker in the area and one of my best friends, helped me find the best independent community for my mom. Melinda has always been more of a sister to me, and the transition would not have gone smoothly without her aid.

My anxiety level went down once we concluded my mother would move to Houston, until it came time to pack up her belongings.

While my mother loves throwing out and giving things away, she treasures hanging on to the past. Some of her possessions made me scratch my head. And I know "people who live in glass houses shouldn't throw stones" since I also have hoarding tendencies and seem to hang on to items from years ago.

However, the difference between my mother's belongings and my own was the lifelong memories. My possessions were mainly simple things of no significance that I probably wouldn't care about if I no longer had them. My mother's treasures had stories to tell, like greeting cards from my father and my sister's college diploma.

"How can I let go of these things?" my mother asked.

"If you get rid of them, you're not throwing away the people. You'll always have the memory," I assured her as she noticeably struggled with each item.

Thankfully, this became our mantra as we went through every drawer and closet in her home. Ultimately, she gave away a lot but still moved more than necessary. But there's comfort in a new place surrounded by familiarity, like all your favorite Lladro, Royal Doulton, and Hummel figurines and other knickknacks from your worldwide travels.

. . .

The time came for me to leave Houston, and my mom, and fly back to New York.

"I feel like I'm dropping you off at college," I said.

"Now you know how I felt when I said goodbye that day," she replied.

Leaving my mom at her new place conjured up all the emotions we shared the day she walked out of my college dorm room and waved goodbye. You only fully appreciate what you put your mother through during your life once the tables turn, and, in a sense, you become the mother.

Will she be okay living in a new place? What happens if she needs me? Will she make new friends? How can I leave her?

The night before I left, I joined my mom in the dining room. Groups of women and men filled the tables, and it felt like walking into a dormitory dining hall. We sat at an empty table since neither of us knew anyone.

"When you come for breakfast tomorrow, I want you to walk up to a table, introduce yourself, and ask to sit with someone new," I said.

"Yes, Mother, I promise I will," she said, laughing.

Fortunately, several friendly women stopped by our table to introduce themselves to us on their way out. At that moment, I knew my mother would be fine.

The irony wasn't lost on me that my tears flowed harder as I walked out and waved goodbye. I'm so blessed to have such an incredible role model who taught me to be a strong, independent woman.

As I left, I felt a sense of calm as I hugged her tight and repeated the exact words she always said to help me through any situation: "You can do this, and always remember, I love you more."

Epilogue

Pandemic Puppy

MORE THAN THIRTY YEARS after declaring I wanted one, I finally got a dog. Of course, I still heard that ex-boyfriend's annoying response when I'd told him I wanted to get one: "You can't even take care of yourself. You're not ready for a dog." Well, I showed him.

The decision to get a family dog was challenging. There were endless back-and-forth conversations about what type of dog would fit our lifestyle and who would care for, walk, and feed it. And the big question: Who would clean up after him? I already knew the answer to the last question: me. I was ready and had been for more than thirty years. But were Adam and Jack?

"Now that we're living full-time in a house with space and a yard, I want a dog. I'm ready," I told Adam and Jack.

"Yes, let's get a dog!" Jack said with enthusiasm.

"I'm glad you're both ready, but I don't think I'm ready for the dog to ruin our new furniture and rugs," Adam said.

In the summer of 2020, we'd lived in our Hamptons house full-time for four months and had spent a fortune decorating and furnishing it. Adam and I had both grown up with dogs, and secretly, I knew he wanted to add a fur baby to our family as much as I did. He eventually stopped worrying about a dog soiling our possessions because I opened my birthday card that August, and inside was a picture of a cute little Yorkshire Terrier.

"What is this?" I asked him.

"It's your birthday present. We're getting a dog," he said.

"This dog?" I asked.

"No. This is only a picture. We'll pick the dog together."

I couldn't stop screaming with excitement. Finally, after all these years of wanting a dog, I'd soon have one.

Then, my search began. I'd always wanted a Yorkshire Terrier, so I scoured the internet, animal shelters, rescue centers, and breeders looking for one. I found nothing. Who knew pandemic puppies would become a trend. I eventually found a local Yorkie breeder and had an hour-long conversation with her.

"I like to screen my potential families because my dogs are my babies, and I don't give them to just anyone. But I like you," she said.

"Thank you," I said carefully. I had this picture in my mind of little Yorkie puppies in tiny cribs all over her house. "When will you have a new litter?"

"Not until later in the year. But I must ask you, have you ever been a pet parent?"

I had to think about this answer. My last dog had been Pepe, a toy poodle, which we'd had to return to the owner because he'd been crazy. Of course, being half toy poodle and half chihuahua, Pepe's temperament had made him more like a Tasmanian devil than a dog, and my dad had relentlessly teased him, which hadn't helped.

"It's been many years, but I love dogs," I cautiously told her, not answering her question directly.

"Do you think you're ready to care for a puppy?" she asked.

Without skipping a beat, I confidently said, "I raised a boy, so, yes, I am."

"Wonderful. I'll put you on my list and be in touch. But I have a long list, so it might not be my next litter."

This led me to a nationwide puppy website that acted as a consortium of breeders. After speaking to a representative to discuss what I wanted, I was pleased when he went to work and sent me pictures of multiple Yorkies.

"Is it weird that we're finding our dog online, the same way we found each other and Jack's nannies and babysitters?" I asked Adam.

After an exhaustive search of Yorkies, we found Toby Jo, a black, brown, and tan little cutie with the sweetest eyes.

"This is our puppy; I want that dog," I said.

Because Toby Jo was only six weeks old, we had to wait a few months to get him. During the interim, I read everything about raising a Yorkshire Terrier puppy and stocked the house with essential items for his arrival.

I told Adam, "There should be a book called "What to Expect When You're Expecting a Puppy."

He laughed.

"Getting ready for Toby's arrival feels like nesting for Jack's birth. Should I ask Melinda to help me prepare like she did for Jack?" I asked.

"At least we have more room in the house, unlike our apartment," Adam said.

My neighbor, Michelle, had two dogs at the time: Shamus, a goldendoodle, and Daisy, a Maltipoo. I frequently consulted her about obedience training, veterinarians, pet stores, grooming, crate training, and everything else.

"There's so much to understand when having a puppy. How will I ever figure it all out?" I asked her.

"You'll be fine. It's like raising a child, but easier, and the dog won't talk back," Michelle said.

Everything I read about Yorkshire Terriers said the standard size for the breed was between six and eight pounds, so we assumed our little puppy would fall into this range. As such, I purchased items for a small dog that fell into the less-than-ten-pounds category: carriers, crates, sweaters, and food and snacks.

"What happens if he's bigger?" Adam asked.

"Well, I also read some Yorkies can be as much as ten to twelve pounds, but many say if your Yorkie is fifteen pounds or more, it's not a Yorkie."

The two months before Toby's arrival went slowly. The anticipation felt like the final two months of my pregnancy. I couldn't wait for him to arrive. One evening, while Adam, Jack, and I were having dinner, I asked about names for the new puppy.

"What will we call the dog? Do we like Toby Jo, or do you have other suggestions?"

"I like Toby, but without Jo," Jack said.

We bounced around a few names like Corky and Joey but collectively agreed on Toby, minus Jo.

. . .

On October 3, 2020, Toby arrived at JFK Airport via the Puppy Express airplane and then by My Pet Cab to his new home in Hampton Bays.

"Of course, our dog would arrive via a private charter and a puppy limo. Only the best for our Toby," I said.

The morning of Toby's drop-off, we went to the local pet store to pick up food, a bed for his new crate, and a puppy gate. The three of us anxiously paced the house, anticipating Toby's arrival.

"I just got a text from the driver. He'll be here in five minutes," I said.

Jack waited at the top of the driveway while Adam and I made last-minute adjustments to the gate and crate. And then the van pulled into the driveway, and we all ran to greet it.

When the driver opened the back of his van, Adam, Jack, and I watched him open the crate carrying Toby. The driver took him out of the carrier and handed Toby to me.

"Well, will you look at that. He likes you," the driver said.

Toby licked my face, and I instantly fell in love.

We let Toby into the house and watched as he cautiously entered each room. Our home has a finished basement with lots of room for Toby to run and explore. It also has several rugs for him to pee and poop on, which he did in those early days and still does from time to time.

Toby's first night in our home arrived, and we put him in his new sleeping quarters. He seemed content until we left the room.

"Is he going to cry all night? How will we ever get to sleep?" I asked Adam.

"You wanted a dog," he said, teasing me.

We eventually got into a routine, and Toby began sleeping through the night.

Jack, Adam, and I spent the crisp fall days after Toby's arrival hiking, going to the beach, and exploring the trails in our neighborhood.

"I thought a Yorkie was supposed to be an indoor dog. He loves to run outside and take long walks as much as a golden retriever," Adam said.

Toby turned out to be anything but a typical Yorkshire Terrier. He tipped the scales at fifteen pounds instead of the standard seven to eight pounds.

"I guess he's not a Yorkie, but he's the best dog ever," I said.

In the days after his arrival, I'd play with Toby during the day, trying to teach him tricks. Like a newborn baby, he'd tire easily and spend hours sleeping in his crate or on my lap. I also took Toby in the car to pick up Jack from school. He'd sit in anticipation of Jack's arrival, staring out the window. And once he saw Jack coming toward the car, he'd jump around, barking with excitement.

Toby quickly became part of our family. I can't imagine our lives without him. He also fits perfectly with all the other neighborhood dogs. Michelle and I regularly walk our dogs together. Since Toby's arrival, she's added another puppy to her brood, Finnegan, an adorable miniature Bernedoodle. Most recently, she had to say goodbye to Shamus, and she added Sonny, another adorable goldendoodle.

"I think Toby needs a friend. Michelle has three dogs," I said to Adam.

"Yes, Toby definitely needs a sibling," Jack said. "Can we please get another dog?"

"One is absolutely enough," Adam said.

While I'd love a playmate for Toby, I agree that one dog is plenty for our family. Why rock the boat?

I finally got my little buddy nearly thirty years after declaring I wanted a dog. I only prayed he'd be easier to raise than Jack. The joy a dog brings to a home is indescribable. Bad days and foul moods melt away with one look into Toby's sweet eyes.

I've always believed that everything in life happens for a reason, even if we don't understand the reason or think our lives should play out differently. I knew I could handle a dog, no matter what that ex-boyfriend thought. And if you're keeping score, I had my baby at forty-three and got my fur baby at fifty-six. I may have been the oldest mom on the playground and late to the party to get a dog, but each was worth the wait.

My life is happy and complete, and looking back, I wouldn't have changed a thing.

Acknowledgments

I WANT TO EXPRESS my deep gratitude to the many people who have supported me on my journey to becoming an author. I am very thankful to those who have been my pillars of strength in the chaotic world of motherhood. This book would not have been possible without the support of many incredible individuals.

I want to thank **Jenna at One Lit Place**, who has been my biggest cheerleader. I am also grateful to **Shasta** for her guidance and encouragement. You continue to make my words sing more than I could ever imagine. I'd also like to thank **Christine**, whose superb mastery of proofreading and the style guide amazes me with every detail. And to **Amy** for her vision. I was able to continue with the memory of you and I hope I made you proud.

I also want to thank the amazing moms in my life who guide and support me every day and keep my sanity in check, including **Melinda, Hannah, Carmen, Jill, Michelle, Cynthia, Alysa, Julie, Shana, and Meridith**. And special thanks to the rock-star moms from Dwight, especially **Tiki, Kathryn, Danny, Nuala, and Emily**. Being surrounded by you makes me feel young—until you start drinking me under the table!

To **Desirée**, I am grateful for everything I have learned about motherhood and myself from you. I cannot imagine our lives without you. You are a fantastic mom!

To my **Zeidman** cousins (**Fred, Kay, Leslie, Mark, Jay, Nancy, and all your spouses and children**), thank you for always supporting me and showing Jack what it means to be a close-knit family. I love you all! And to Mark and Sarah, I am here for any midlife parenting tips you may need!

To **Adam**, there aren't enough words to describe how thankful and grateful I am for you. Not every day is perfect, and NOTHING is easy. Still, I'll always appreciate having you as my partner in life and parenthood. I love you!

To **Jack**, it goes without saying that if not for you, there would be no book. If I've said it once, I've said it a million times—you are my whole world, and I will always love you more!

To my **mom**, thank you for being the best role model and showing me how to be a good mother. Your unwavering love and support have been my anchor. I aspire to be as good a mother to Jack as you have been to me. Your respect for my choices and belief in my abilities have given me the confidence to navigate the wild world of motherhood. I love you!

Finally, big thanks to **you, the readers**, who take the time to immerse yourself in my writing and return for more. Thank you for letting me entertain you and officially making me an author!